The Vegetarian and Vegan Gluten-Free Cookbook

Sarah Lee Anniston

Printed in the United States of America

ISBN 978-1470082383

Table Of Contents

Introduction

When I was diagnosed with celiac disease in 2008, I had been a vegan for three years and a vegetarian for 30. Imagine my horror when I discovered that 99 percent of vegan meat substitutes (the soy-based sausages, the wheat-based patties) were not gluten-free. My doctor recommended I eat fish, and after talking to several other former vegetarians who were diagnosed with celiac and "had to" start eating meat again, I realized it was going to be an uphill battle to remain vegetarian, let alone vegan.

Four years later, I'm healthier than I have ever been (I have the blood work to prove it) and I'm still proudly vegetarian. While I do eat some dairy and free range eggs, I balance my diet with completely vegan meals using beans and rice as complete proteins. I also use tofu hamburger crumbles (there's only one brand that I've found – Marjan – that is gluten-free) and Quorn "chicken" patties: actually a type of fungus. The recipes you'll find in this book use a combination of many different proteins, and about half are completely vegan – that is, free of all animal products.

The one thing I have learned in the last four years is to read, read, read labels. I've recommended certain brands that I use for many recipes. I don't endorse any particular brand per se, but the brands I have included are gluten-free. If you do choose another brand, make sure to check the label to make sure the product is gluten-free. Most recipes contain readily available ingredients like fresh produce. There are a few unusual products but they can normally be found in larger grocery stores that have a green or natural food section, like Publix. Alternatively, Whole Foods is a haven for gluten-free products. You can also purchase nearly all of these products at Amazon.com's grocery store, although you'll have to buy in bulk. That's where I shop, so if you see an unusual ingredient in a recipe (like Sriracha hot sauce), check out

Amazon.com. You'll probably find the product there. Celiac.com and GlutenFree.com also have a wide variety of gluten-free products.

IAs a gluten-free vegetarian, purchasing online has been a convenient and inexpensive way for me to find gluten-free products like hot sauces and pastas. If you join the Amazon Prime shipping club ($79 per year), you get free two day shipping all year and the products are generally a dollar or two cheaper than regular stores.

Bragg's liquid aminos is a gluten free soy sauce replacement.

Besan is a type of flour made from chick peas. You'll find it in Indian grocery stores.

Agave nectar is a sweetener obtained from the cactus plant. It's gaining in popularity – most stores carry it now.

Rice tortillas can be found in the freezer section of natural health food stores.

Getting enough protein in your diet can be a challenge if you are vegetarian and gluten-free. Cheese, milk, and eggs are used in some (but not all) of the recipes in the vegetarian sections. Beans and rice are staples for several other recipes and many others rely on the protein naturally found in vegetables like spinach and peas. The following products are used in a few recipes:

Quorn is a type of manufactured protein, similar to mushrooms. It's high in protein and can be purchased from the freezer section of many large grocery stores. At the time of writing, only the patties (which resemble chicken breasts) are gluten-free.

Marjon vegetarian hamburger tofu crumbles resemble ground beef and can usually be found in the refrigerated health food section of larger grocery stores, alongside other vegetarian products like vegetarian bacon and hot dogs.

The Vegetarian and Vegan Gluten Free Cookbook
Introduction

Vegan Breakfast

Fruit Smoothie

2 Tbsp Flax seeds (soaked 3 hours)

1 cup cashews (soaked 3 hours)

4 cups water

1 Banana

1 cup mixed berries

2 cups spinach, uncooked

¼ cup dates (soaked 3 hours)

1 cup ice

Procedure

1   Combine all ingredients in a blender and blend until smooth.

Servings: 4

Yield: 4

Preparation Time: 5 minutes

Nutrition Facts

Serving size: 1
smoothie

Amount Per Serving	
Calories	387.12
Calories From Fat (26%)	99.59
	% Daily Value
Total Fat 11.9g	18%
Saturated Fat 1.67g	8%
Cholesterol 0mg	0%
Sodium 48.01mg	2%
Potassium 884.19mg	25%
Total Carbohydrates 69.29g	23%
Fiber 10.09g	40%
Sugar 22.46g	
Protein 8.6g	17%

Recipe Type

Breakfast

Granola Bars

Make these on Sunday and they will last for a week in the fridge.

1-2 apples

1 ½ cups pitted dates (soaked for 3 hours)

½ cup agave nectar

2 Tbsp lemon juice, fresh

2 Tbsp orange extract or zest

1 Tbsp vanilla extract

1 tsp ground cinnamon

2 tsp sea salt

7 cups mixed raw nuts (coarsely chopped) and seeds soaked   overnight and rinsed well (walnuts, almonds, sunflower   seeds, etc)

1 cup dried cranberries (apple juice sweetened)

Procedure

Preheat oven to 350 degrees F. In food processor, place apples, dates, agave, lemon juice, orange zest, vanilla, cinnamon, salt, and process until completely smooth. Transfer to a large bowl.

Add nuts and seeds. Mix well.

Spread on a baking sheet and bake until crunchy (about 20 minutes).

Yield: 10 cups or 40 bars

Nutrition Facts

Serving size: 1 bar

Amount Per Serving	
Calories	231.14
Calories From Fat (46%)	106.37
	% Daily Value
Total Fat 12.67g	19%
Saturated Fat 1.66g	8%
Cholesterol 0mg	0%
Sodium 1097.4mg	46%
Potassium 201.4mg	6%
Total Carbohydrates 27.86g	9%
Fiber 3.86g	15%
Sugar 8.13g	
Protein 4.41g	9%

Spanish Scrambler Wrap

2 Tbsp olive oil	1 tsp ground cumin
1 cup red and green bell pepper, chopped	1 tsp turmeric
	1 pound fresh spinach
1 small onion chopped	1/2 cup salsa
12 oz extra-firm tofu, crumbled	4 (8 inch) rice tortillas
1/2 cup vegetable broth	
1 tsp chili powder	

Procedure

1   Heat olive oil over medium heat in a skillet. Add the bell pepper and onion and sauté until onion is translucent.

2   Add the tofu, 1/4 cup broth, chili powder, cumin and turmeric. Sauté stirring often, for 5 to 7 min, until lightly brown. Add spinach and remaining 1/4 cup broth and cook 1 min until spinach has wilted.

3   Add salsa and stir.

4   Divide the tofu mixture evenly among the tortillas and roll up the filling.

Servings: 4

Yield: 4

Preparation Time: 5 minutes

Cooking Time: 22 minutes

Nutrition Facts

Serving size: 1/4 of a recipe (15 ounces).

Amount Per Serving	
Calories	224.73
Calories From Fat (52%)	116.89
	% Daily Value
Total Fat 13.57g	21%
Saturated Fat 1.62g	8%
Cholesterol 0.31mg	<1%
Sodium 783.54mg	33%
Potassium 724.71mg	21%
Total Carbohydrates 16.7g	6%
Fiber 6.77g	27%
Sugar 3.69g	
Protein 14.93g	30%

Recipe Type

Breakfast

Vegetarian Breakfast

Tofu Scramble

Think tofu is bland? You'll be surprised by this recipe, which resembles scrambled eggs. This recipe can be made vegan by substituting vegan cheese.

2 Tbsp olive oil
1 green bell pepper, seeded and chopped
1 small onion chopped
1/2 cup sliced mushrooms
12 oz extra-firm tofu, drained and pressed

1 Tbsp nutritional yeast
1 tsp turmeric
1/2 tsp freshly ground black pepper
4 slices American cheese slices

Procedure

1. Heat 2T olive oil in a saucepan over medium heat. Add the onion, pepper and mushrooms. Sauté for 4-5 minutes until onion is translucent.
2. Add the tofu and then stir often for 5 to 7 min. Add the nutritional yeast, turmeric, and black pepper and stir well.
3. Top with cheese.

Servings: 4
Yield: 4
Preparation Time: 15 minutes
Cooking Time: 10 minutes

Nutrition Facts

Serving size: 1/4 of a recipe (6.9 ounces).

Amount Per Serving	
Calories	255.17
Calories From Fat (65%)	165.93
	% Daily Value
Total Fat 19.11g	29%
Saturated Fat 5.98g	30%
Cholesterol 18.7mg	6%
Sodium 466.89mg	19%
Potassium 339.19mg	10%
Total Carbohydrates 8.9g	3%
Fiber 1.56g	6%
Sugar 4.78g	
Protein 14.94g	30%

Recipe Type

Breakfast

Irish Eggs

2 Tbsp olive oil
2 large potatoes peeled and diced into 1/4" chunks
1 onion minced
1/2 teaspoon turmeric

1 teaspoon chili powder
1 green bell pepper, chopped
6 eggs beaten

Procedure

1   In a large skillet, warm olive oil over medium low heat. Add potatoes, onion and green pepper. Cover pan; sauté until potatoes are browned (about 15 minutes). Stir frequently.
2   Add turmeric and chili powder. Stir well.
3   Push potatoes to one side of pan. Add eggs to pan and then scramble until done. Mix with potatoes and serve.

Servings: 4
Yield: 4
Preparation Time: 15 minutes
Cooking Time: 20 minutes
Total Time: 35 minutes

Nutrition Facts

Serving size: 1/4 of a recipe (8.6 ounces).

Amount Per Serving	
Calories	255.09
Calories From Fat (47%)	118.97
	% Daily Value
Total Fat 13.38g	21%
Saturated Fat 6.11g	31%
Cholesterol 294.27mg	98%
Sodium 148.02mg	6%
Potassium 646.58mg	18%
Total Carbohydrates 22.33g	7%
Fiber 3.91g	16%
Sugar 3.32g	
Protein 12.28g	25%

Recipe Type

Breakfast Foods

Oven Omelet

8 eggs
1 cup milk
2 cups shredded hash brown potatoes
1 cup finely chopped red bell pepper
1 cup shredded Cheddar cheese
salt and pepper to taste

Procedure

1 Preheat oven to 350 degrees F (175 degrees C). Lightly grease an 8x8 inch glass baking dish.

2 Beat eggs in a large bowl; stir in the milk. Stir in the potatoes, red pepper and cheese. Season to taste and pour into prepared pan.

3 Bake in preheated oven for 45 to 50 minutes, until knife inserted in middle comes out clean.

Servings: 7
Yield: 6-8
Preparation Time: 5 minutes
Cooking Time: 45 minutes
Total Time: 50 minutes

Nutrition Facts

Serving size: 1/7 of a recipe (6.8 ounces).

Amount Per Serving	
Calories	220.18
Calories From Fat (48%)	105.84
	% Daily Value
Total Fat 11.91g	18%
Saturated Fat 5.73g	29%
Cholesterol 232.31mg	77%
Sodium 236.32mg	10%
Potassium 359.52mg	10%
Total Carbohydrates 14.35g	5%
Fiber 1.24g	5%
Sugar 3.07g	
Protein 13.81g	28%

Recipe Type

Breakfast Foods

13

Spinach Frittata

1 bag spinach	16 oz extra-firm tofu, crumbled
1/4 cup milk	1/8 tsp turmeric
1/3 cup vegetable broth	1/4 tsp salt
2 medium potatoes peeled and chopped into 1/4-inch cubes	1/4 tsp freshly ground black pepper
2 garlic cloves, minced	1/4 tsp chili powder

Procedure

1   Preheat the oven to 375 degrees F.

2   Sauté spinach in a large pan on medium heat with the milk and vegetable broth until the spinach wilts – about two minutes. Add potatoes and garlic. Cover pan. Cook on medium low until potatoes are soft, about 15 minutes. Stir frequently.

3   Puree half the tofu with turmeric, salt, black pepper and chili powder in a food processor. Crumble the other half. Combine all ingredients and mix well. Place in a 6-inch x 6-inch baking dish and bake for 20 min. Remove the frittata from the oven and allow it to set for at least 10 min before serving.

Servings: 8
Yield: 8
Preparation Time: 10 minutes
Cooking Time: 20 minutes

Nutrition Facts

Serving size: 1/8 of a recipe (6.5 ounces).

Amount Per Serving	
Calories	113.92
Calories From Fat (28%)	31.38
	% Daily Value
Total Fat 3.75g	6%
Saturated Fat 0.4g	2%
Cholesterol 0.1mg	<1%
Sodium 157.39mg	7%
Potassium 637.07mg	18%
Total Carbohydrates 13.92g	5%
Fiber 2.83g	11%
Sugar 0.95g	
Protein 8.62g	17%

Recipe Type

Breakfast

Sweet Potato Hash

2 pounds sweet potatoes peeled and cut into 1/4-inch pieces
4 tbsp olive oil
3 garlic cloves, chopped
1 small onion chopped
1 small red bell pepper, chopped
1 small green bell pepper, chopped
1 Tbsp sweet paprika
kosher or sea salt to taste
Freshly ground black pepper to taste
6 eggs beaten

Procedure

1   Place sweet potatoes with water to cover in a large saucepan. Simmer potatoes for about 15 to 17 min until just tender. Drain and set aside.

2   Heat 2T oil in a large skillet over medium heat. Cook garlic, onion and bell peppers for about 4 min. Add paprika, salt and black pepper and continue to cook for 5 min. until vegetable are soft. Add the sweet potatoes and cook to heat through.

3   Heat a separate pan over medium heat and scramble the eggs in the remaining olive oil.

4   Stir all ingredients together.

Servings: 6
Yield: 6
Preparation Time: 15 minutes
Cooking Time: 35 minutes

Nutrition Facts

Serving size: 1/6 of a recipe (10.1 ounces).

Amount Per Serving	
Calories	274.33
Calories From Fat (32%)	87.17
	% Daily Value
Total Fat 9.78g	15%
Saturated Fat 2.3g	12%
Cholesterol 186.1mg	62%
Sodium 272.56mg	11%
Potassium 751.42mg	21%
Total Carbohydrates 37.55g	13%
Fiber 6.4g	26%
Sugar 9.1g	
Protein 9.84g	20%

Recipe Type

Breakfast

Vegan Dinners

Oriental Grilled Tofu Steaks

2 (1 pound) block extra firm low fat tofu
1 cup vegetable broth
3 Tbsp Bragg's liquid aminos
1 Tbsp Kame or Dynasty brand hoisin sauce
1 Tbsp Spice Island cooking sherry
1 Tbsp agave nectar
2 cloves garlic, minced

1 Tbsp fresh ginger, grated
1 tsp orange zest
1 tsp cornstarch
 Vegetable oil cooking spray
 20 wooden skewers, soaked for 1 hr in warm water
1/4 cup scallions, sliced for garnish

Procedure

1   Slice the tofu into 3/4 inch slices.

2   Whisk together broth, Bragg's, hoisin sauce, sherry, agave nectar, garlic, ginger and orange zest in a medium bowl. Arrange tofu in a shallow baking dish. Pour marinade over tofu and marinate, covered, in the refrigerator for 2 hrs.

3   Remove tofu from baking dish. Place marinade in a saucepan and bring to a boil. In a small bowl, combine cornstarch with 2 tsp water and whisk. Add to marinade and cook until thickened, about 1 min. Set aside.

4   Using 2 skewers per slice of tofu spaced evenly, slide the skewers through the tofu, with only the tips of the skewers extending through one end of the tofu.

5   Place the tofu on a foil-lined pan and baste with some of the reserved marinade. Broil the tofu for 4 minutes. Turn, baste and grill tofu for another 4 min, continuing to baste with reserved marinade. Remove tofu to a platter and drizzle with any remaining sauce. Sprinkle with scallions.

Servings: 5
Yield: 5
Preparation Time: 4 hours
Cooking Time: 15 minutes

Nutrition Facts

Serving size:
1/5 of a recipe
(3.7 ounces).

Amount Per Serving	
Calories	44.7
Calories From Fat (16%)	7.19
	% Daily Value
Total Fat 0.8g	1%
Saturated Fat 0.12g	<1%
Cholesterol 0mg	0%
Sodium 132.67mg	6%
Potassium 81.02mg	2%
Total Carbohydrates 6.28g	2%
Fiber 0.27g	1%
Sugar 4.33g	
Protein 2.7g	5%

Recipe Type

Grilled, Main Dish

Black Beans and Rice

A Mexican staple, the combination of black beans and rice provides a complete protein. Top with chopped lettuce, tomato salsa, and avocado for a filling dish.

2 Tbsp olive oil
1/4 cup shallots finely chopped
2 tsp garlic, minced
1/4 tsp ground cumin
1 1/3 cup vegetable broth
2/3 cup brown rice, rinsed

2 Tbsp fresh cilantro, finely chopped
2 Tbsp finely chopped scallions
1 (15 oz) can black beans, drained and rinsed
kosher or sea salt to taste
Ground black pepper to taste

Procedure

1   Sauté shallots and garlic in olive oil for 3 min. Add cumin and sauté for 2 min.

2   Add broth and rice and bring to a boil. Cover and simmer on low heat for about 45 min., or until rice is tender. Add cilantro, scallions, beans, salt and black pepper and mix well.

Servings: 4
Yield: 4
Preparation Time: 10 minutes
Cooking Time: 50 minutes

Nutrition Facts

Serving size: 1/4 of a recipe (11.6 ounces).

Amount Per Serving	
Calories	193.37
Calories From Fat (6%)	10.72
	% Daily Value
Total Fat 1.3g	2%
Saturated Fat 0.07g	<1%
Cholesterol 0mg	0%
Sodium 725.05mg	30%
Potassium 209.37mg	6%
Total Carbohydrates 42.48g	14%
Fiber 5.94g	24%
Sugar 2.09g	
Protein 6.27g	13%

Recipe Type

Filling, Main Dish

Black Bean Enchiladas

8 oz tomato sauce
½ cup water
⅛ tsp ground cumin
3 Tbsp picante sauce
1 ½ tsp chili powder
12 oz Marjon vegetarian hamburger tofu crumbles
1 tsp dry onion soup mix
½ cup low-sodium canned black beans, drained
¼ cup finely chopped onion
2 Tbsp chopped fresh cilantro
½ cup "Cheese" Sauce (see recipe on next page)
6 Corn tortillas
4 oz grated vegan cheese

Procedure

Stir the tomato sauce, water, cumin, picante, and chili powder together in a medium saucepan. Heat through and simmer for 5 minutes.

Add the crumbles and heat for an additional 5 minutes.

Add onion soup mix, beans, onion, cilantro, and ¼ cup of cheese sauce. Mix well.

Preheat oven to 350°F.

Place the tortillas in a microwave for 15-20 seconds to soften.

Divide the filling and fill each tortilla, folding the tortilla underneath.

Pour cheese sauce on top of enchiladas.

Top with grated cheese.

Bake for 15 minutes until the cheese has melted and the enchiladas are heated through.

Yield: 6 servings

Nutrition Facts

Serving size: 1/6 of a recipe (9.3 ounces).

Amount Per Serving	
Calories	363.84
Calories From Fat (23%)	82.87
	% Daily Value
Total Fat 9.27g	14%
Saturated Fat 1.53g	8%
Cholesterol 0mg	0%
Sodium 1627.48mg	68%
Potassium 592.55mg	17%
Total Carbohydrates 37.36g	12%
Fiber 8.82g	35%
Sugar 3.91g	
Protein 33.1g	66%

"Cheese" Sauce

1 ¼ cups water
¼ cup raw cashew pieces
1 Tbsp nutritional yeast flakes
1 cup frozen, cooked brown rice
1 tsp salt
¼ tsp garlic powder
1 tsp onion powder
1 ½ Tbsp lemon juice

Procedure

Blend all the ingredients in a food processor or blender until creamy, about 5 minutes.

Yield: 8 Servings

Nutrition Facts

Serving size: 1/8 of a recipe (2.4 ounces).

Amount Per Serving	
Calories	37.8
Calories From Fat (13%)	4.98
	% Daily Value
Total Fat 0.59g	<1%
Saturated Fat 0.11g	<1%
Cholesterol 0mg	0%
Sodium 373.36mg	16%
Potassium 91.38mg	3%
Total Carbohydrates 6.82g	2%
Fiber 0.57g	2%
Sugar 0.25g	
Protein 1.41g	3%

Mild Curry Tofu

2 bunches green onions
1 (14 oz) can light coconut milk
1/4 cup Bragg's liquid aminos, divided
1/2 tsp agave nectar
1 1/2 tsp curry powder
1 tsp minced fresh ginger
2 tsp Sriracha Hot Chili Sauce
1 pound firm tofu cut into 3/4 inch cubes
4 roma (plum) tomatoes, chopped
1 yellow bell pepper, thinly sliced
4 oz fresh mushrooms, chopped
1/4 cup chopped fresh basil
4 cups chopped bok choy
 salt to taste

Procedure

1　　Finely chop green onions.

2　　In a large heavy skillet over medium heat, mix coconut milk, 3 tablespoons Bragg's, agave, curry powder, ginger, and chili sauce. Bring to a boil.

3　　Stir tofu, tomatoes, yellow pepper, mushrooms, and finely chopped green onions into the skillet. Cover, and cook 5 minutes, stirring occasionally. Mix in basil and bok choy. Add salt and remaining Bragg's. Continue cooking 5 minutes, or until vegetables are tender.

Servings: 6
Yield: 6
Preparation Time: 25 minutes
Cooking Time: 15 minutes
Total Time: 40 minutes

Nutrition Facts

Serving size: 1/6 of a recipe (11.4 ounces).

Amount Per Serving	
Calories	128.4
Calories From Fat (33%)	42.27
	% Daily Value
Total Fat 5.06g	8%
Saturated Fat 0.55g	3%
Cholesterol 0mg	0%
Sodium 452.92mg	19%
Potassium 741.94mg	21%
Total Carbohydrates 13.69g	5%
Fiber 4.51g	18%
Sugar 5.07g	
Protein 11.71g	23%

Recipe Type
Dinner

Curried Vegetables

1 tbsp olive oil
1 large onion chopped
4 cloves garlic, minced
2 Tbsp fresh ginger, minced
1 jalapeño pepper, chopped
2/3 cup tomato puree
1 tsp ground coriander
1 tsp ground cumin

1/4 tsp turmeric
1/4 cup chopped fresh cilantro
1 Tbsp Bragg's liquid aminos
2 small sweet potatoes, peeled and cut into 1/4-inch cubes
1/2 head cauliflower, separated into florets
2 cups frozen green peas, thawed

Procedure

1   Heat oil in a large skillet over medium heat. Put in the onion, garlic, ginger and pepper. Sauté for 5 min. Stir in 3 tbsp water and cook for 3 min.

2   Stir in tomato puree, coriander, cumin, turmeric, cilantro, Bragg's, and sweet potatoes. Cover skillet. Cook for 15 min. Stir frequently.

3   Add the cauliflower, cover and simmer for 15 to 20 min. Add peas and cook for 5 additional min.

Servings: 4
Yield: 4
Preparation Time: 20 minutes
Cooking Time: 45 minutes

Nutrition Facts

Serving size: 1/4 of a recipe (9.3 ounces).

Amount Per Serving	
Calories	140.65
Calories From Fat (4%)	5.74
	% Daily Value
Total Fat 0.69g	1%
Saturated Fat 0.11g	<1%
Cholesterol 0mg	0%
Sodium 314.05mg	13%
Potassium 657.08mg	19%
Total Carbohydrates 30.42g	10%
Fiber 6.89g	28%
Sugar 9.42g	
Protein 5.58g	11%

Recipe Type

Vegetables

Grilled Portobello Mushroom

6 medium Portobello mushrooms
6 cloves garlic minced
6 Tbsp lemon juice
6 Tbsp balsamic vinegar
3 Tbsp chopped fresh basil

1 Tbsp garlic minced
kosher or sea salt to taste
Freshly ground black pepper to taste
Vegetable oil cooking spray

Procedure

1   Remove stems from mushrooms and discard. Rinse mushroom caps to remove any surface dirt.

2   Tuck garlic into the gills of the mushrooms. Space out so the entire mushroom has garlic divided throughout.

3   Place mushrooms in a large baking pan. Mix together the lemon juice, vinegar, basil, minced garlic, salt and black pepper. Pour over the mushrooms and let marinate for 1-2 hrs.

4   Remove the mushrooms from the marinade. Coat a grill rack with cooking spray. Grill the mushrooms over medium-high heat, turning once, about 2 to 3 min per side, basting with any leftover marinade.

Servings: 6
Preparation Time: 2 hours
Cooking Time: 10 minutes

Nutrition Facts

Serving size: 1/6 of a recipe (4.4 ounces).

Amount Per Serving	
Calories	50.08
Calories From Fat (10%)	4.84
	% Daily Value
Total Fat 0.57g	<1%
Saturated Fat 0.13g	<1%
Cholesterol 0mg	0%
Sodium 61.12mg	3%
Potassium 426.66mg	12%
Total Carbohydrates 9.84g	3%
Fiber 2.15g	9%
Sugar 5.01g	
Protein 2.78g	6%

Recipe Type
Grilled

Moroccan Stew

I make this soup in a crock pot. Simply place all ingredients in the pot and cook on low for 6-8 hours. If you want to follow the directions to make the soup on a stove, you should add 1T olive oil to the ingredients list. If you are vegetarian and prefer a creamy soup, add a tablespoon of warm, heavy cream for each serving.

1/2 cinnamon stick
1 tsp ground cumin
1/2 tsp ground ginger
1/4 tsp ground cloves
1/4 tsp ground nutmeg
1/4 tsp ground turmeric
2 tsp curry powder
1 tsp kosher salt
1/2 sweet onion chopped
1 cup finely shredded kale
2 cans 14 oz organic vegetable broth

1 14.5 oz diced tomatoes, undrained
1 Tbsp agave nectar
2 large carrots, chopped
1 sweet potatoes, peeled and diced
2 large potatoes, peeled and diced
1 can 15 oz garbanzo beans, drained
1/4 cup chopped dried apricots
1/2 cup dried lentils, rinsed
1/2 tsp Ground black pepper, to taste
1 Tbsp cornstarch (optional)
1 Tbsp water (optional)

Procedure

1   Combine cinnamon, cumin, ginger, cloves, nutmeg, turmeric, curry powder, and salt in a large bowl, reserve.

2   Warm olive oil in a large pot over medium heat. Cook the onion in the butter until soft and just beginning to brown, 5 to 10 minutes. Stir in the shredded kale and reserved spice mixture. Cook for 2 minutes or until kale begins to wilt and spices are fragrant.

3   Pour the vegetable broth into the pot. Stir in the tomatoes, agave, carrots, sweet potatoes, potatoes, garbanzo beans, dried apricots, and lentils. Bring to boil; reduce heat to low.

4   Simmer stew for 30 minutes or until the vegetables and lentils are cooked and tender. Season with black pepper to taste. If desired, combine optional cornstarch and water; stir into stew. Simmer until stew has thickened, about 5 minutes.

Servings: 6
Yield: 6
Preparation Time: 30 minutes
Cooking Time: 40 minutes
Total Time: 1 hour and 10 minutes

Nutrition Facts

Serving size:
1/6 of a recipe
(10.6 ounces).

Amount Per Serving	
Calories	543
Calories From Fat (7%)	36.77
	% Daily Value
Total Fat 4.2g	6%
Saturated Fat 1.5g	8%
Cholesterol 5mg	2%
Sodium 1218mg	51%
Potassium 2046mg	58%
Total Carbohydrates 110.6g	37%
Fiber 24g	96%
Sugar 23.2g	
Protein 19.5g	39%

Recipe Type

Vegetable stew

Roasted Eggplant and Red Pepper Salad

1 pound eggplant
2 red bell pepper
2 tomatoes seeded
and chopped
2 cloves garlic,
minced
1/4 cup finely chopped
red onion
1/4 cup fresh parsley,
finely chopped

2 tsp red wine vinegar
2 tsp Dijon mustard
1/2 tsp agave nectar
kosher or sea salt to
taste
Freshly ground black
pepper to taste

Procedure

1   Preheat the oven to 400°F. Cut the eggplant in half and remove the stem, seeds and membrane. Place the eggplant and peppers on a baking sheet covered with parchment paper and roast for about 25 to 30 min until soft. Place the peppers in a bowl and cover with plastic wrap, until cool enough to handle.

2   Peel the skin off the peppers and cut into strips. Scoop out the flesh of the eggplant and mash, and then drain any extra liquid.

3   Place the peppers and eggplant in a large bowl. Add the tomatoes, garlic, onion and parsley. Mix together the vinegar, mustard, agave, salt and black pepper in a small bowl. Pour the dressing onto the salad and mix well. Cover and refrigerate for at least 1 hour prior to serving.

Servings: 6
Preparation Time: 10 minutes
Cooking Time: 50 minutes

Nutrition Facts

Serving size: 1/6 of a recipe (5.9 ounces).

Amount Per Serving	
Calories	45.48
Calories From Fat (9%)	4.01
	% Daily Value
Total Fat 0.48g	<1%
Saturated Fat 0.05g	<1%
Cholesterol 0mg	0%
Sodium 75.55mg	3%
Potassium 355.9mg	10%
Total Carbohydrates 9.7g	3%
Fiber 4.15g	17%
Sugar 3.93g	
Protein 1.75g	4%

Recipe Type

Salad

Pepper and Zucchini Fettuccini

1 large red bell pepper
1 large yellow bell pepper
2 tbsp olive oil
1 large onion, halved and sliced
3 garlic clove minced
2 medium zucchini, sliced into 1/4 inch thick rounds
pinch crushed red pepper

1/2 cup dry white wine
1 Tbsp lemon juice
2 tsp fresh thyme
1 pinch sea salt
 Freshly ground black pepper to taste
1 (10 oz) package Tinkyada gluten free fettuccini
1/4 cup vegan Parmesan cheese

Procedure

1   Cut the peppers in half and remove the seeds and white membrane. Place the pepper halves on a broiler pan. Broil the peppers skin-side up until the skin blackens. Place the pepper halves in a bowl, cover with plastic wrap and allow to cool.

2   Remove the blackened skin and cut each pepper into 4 pieces. Discard the seeds, skin and white membrane. Cut the peppers into 1-inch strips and set aside.

3   Heat the olive oil in a large skillet over medium heat. Add garlic and onion and sauté for 6 min. Add the zucchini and crushed red pepper and sauté over low heat for 15 min. Add the roasted peppers, wine, lemon juice, thyme, salt and pepper. Sauté for 1 min.

4   Cook the fettuccine according to package directions. Drain the pasta, immediately toss with the vegetable mixture, sprinkle with Parmesan cheese and then serve.

Servings: 4
Yield: 4
Preparation Time: 15 minutes
Cooking Time: 50 minutes

Nutrition Facts

Serving size: 1/4 of a recipe (10.2 ounces).

Amount Per Serving	
Calories	191.99
Calories From Fat (12%)	22.97
	% Daily Value
Total Fat 2.61g	4%
Saturated Fat 1.11g	6%
Cholesterol 3.75mg	1%
Sodium 272.01mg	11%
Potassium 594.48mg	17%
Total Carbohydrates 33.83g	11%
Fiber 3.86g	15%
Sugar 6.07g	
Protein 8.14g	16%

Recipe Type

Pasta

Seasoned Chili fries

1 potato	1/2 tsp garlic powder
1 Tbsp olive oil	1/2 tsp chili powder
1/2 tsp paprika	1/2 tsp onion

Procedure

1. Slice potato thinly, about1/4 inch in diameter
2. Combine ingredients in a large freezer bag and shake well
3. Spread on a cookie sheet and bake at 450 degrees for 20-25 minutes, until slightly blackened at the edges.

Servings: 1
Yield: 1

Nutrition Facts

Serving size: Entire recipe (7.3 ounces).

Amount Per Serving	
Calories	275.2
Calories From Fat (45%)	123.72
	% Daily Value
Total Fat 14.02g	22%
Saturated Fat 1.98g	10%
Cholesterol 0mg	0%
Sodium 35.36mg	1%
Potassium 853.11mg	24%
Total Carbohydrates 35.03g	12%
Fiber 5.14g	21%
Sugar 1.9g	
Protein 4.37g	9%

Stuffed Peppers

1 cup brown basmati rice
4 medium red bell peppers
2 medium yellow bell peppers
2 tbsp olive oil
1 cup chopped onion
1 tsp chili powder
1 tsp ground cumin

1 tsp dried oregano
1/4 tsp sea salt
1/4 tsp ground black pepper
1 (15 oz) can pinto beans, drained
and rinsed
1 cup seeded and chopped tomato
8 slices Cheddar cheese

Procedure

1 Cook rice according to package directions.
2 Preheat the oven to 400°F.
3 Cut each bell pepper in half lengthwise. Remove seeds and ribs. Bring a large saucepan of water to a boil. Add the bell pepper halves and blanch for about 4 min. Drain and pat dry.
4 Heat the oil in a skillet over medium heat. Add the onion and sauté for about 3 min. Add chili powder, cumin, oregano, salt and black pepper. Sauté for 1 min. Add the beans, rice and tomato and sauté for 2 min.
5 Stuffed bell peppers with the mixture, packing them well. Top each bell pepper with a slice of cheese. Place in an 8x8-inch baking dish.
6 Bake bell peppers, uncovered for about 20 min.
7 Set oven to a broil. Broil bell peppers for 1 to 2 min., until the top is browned and cheese is bubbly.

Servings: 4
Yield: 4
Preparation Time: 15 minutes
Cooking Time: 30 minutes

Nutrition Facts

Serving size: 1/4 of a recipe (17 ounces).

Amount Per Serving	
Calories	562.63
Calories From Fat (34%)	190.41
	% Daily Value
Total Fat 21.74g	33%
Saturated Fat 12.19g	61%
Cholesterol 59.65mg	20%
Sodium 2028.49mg	85%
Potassium 880.78mg	25%
Total Carbohydrates 73.26g	24%
Fiber 12.13g	49%
Sugar 8.49g	
Protein 24.63g	49%

Recipe Type
Vegetables

Sweet Potato and Green Pea Curry over Brown Rice

1 cup long grain brown rice
1 tsp ground cumin
1 tsp ground coriander
1 tbsp olive oil
2 1/2 cups vegetable broth

1/4 cup chopped onion
2 cloves garlic minced
2 small sweet potatoes peeled and cut into 1/4-inch cubes

1 tsp turmeric
2 tsp grated lemon zest
1 (10 oz) package frozen baby green peas, thawed
2 Tbsp chopped fresh cilantro
1 pinch sea salt
1 pinch black pepper

Procedure

1   Cook rice according to package directions.
2   Place cumin and coriander in a dry skillet over medium heat and then shake over medium heat until fragrant.
3   Heat 1/4 cup broth in a large saucepan. Add the onion and garlic and cook for 2 min. Add the potatoes and broth and bring to a boil. Cover and lower heat to medium low. Cook until the potatoes are tender, about 12 to 15 min. Add lemon zest and peas. Cook, uncovered for 3 min. Add cilantro, salt and black pepper. Serve over rice.

Servings: 4
Yield: 4
Preparation Time: 10 minutes
Cooking Time: 30 minutes

Nutrition Facts

Serving size: 1/4 of a recipe (11.6 ounces).

Amount Per Serving	
Calories	270.85
Calories From Fat (6%)	15.44
	% Daily Value
Total Fat 1.84g	3%
Saturated Fat 0.35g	2%
Cholesterol 0mg	0%
Sodium 764.05mg	32%
Potassium 471.97mg	13%
Total Carbohydrates 57.52g	19%
Fiber 5.62g	22%
Sugar 6.99g	
Protein 6.59g	13%

Recipe Type

Main Dish, Vegetables

Vegetarian Chili

1 bag Marjon vegetarian hamburger tofu crumbles
46 oz tomato juice
1 can (15 oz) tomato sauce
1 1/2 cup chopped onion
1/2 cup chopped celery
1/4 cup chopped green bell pepper
1/4 cup chili powder
2 tsp cumin

1 1/2 tsp garlic powder
1 tsp salt
1/2 tsp black pepper
1/2 tsp dried oregano
1/2 tsp xylitol
1/8 tsp cayenne pepper, ground
2 cups canned beans

Procedure

1   Combine ingredients and cook for 4 hours in a slow cooker on "high".

Servings: 8
Yield: 8

Nutrition Facts

Serving size: 1/8 of a recipe (12.2 ounces).

Amount Per Serving	
Calories	173.96
Calories From Fat (12%)	20.88
	% Daily Value
Total Fat 2.4g	4%
Saturated Fat 0.35g	2%
Cholesterol 0mg	0%
Sodium 968.7mg	40%
Potassium 938.84mg	27%
Total Carbohydrates 29.34g	10%
Fiber 8.71g	35%
Sugar 10.7g	
Protein 12.54g	25%

Recipe Type

Vegetables

Author Notes

"So good, my meat-eating friends don't believe it's vegetarian"

Vegetarian Dinners

Nacho Salad

For guacamole:
1   small avocado
1 ½ cups silken tofu, soft
¼ tsp salt
1 pinch black pepper
1 pinch cayenne pepper
¼ tsp garlic clove, minced
⅛ tsp cumin
2 Tbsp lemon juice

For nachos:
3 cups baked, whole-grain tortilla chips
4 cups iceberg lettuce, shredded
1 can black beans, drained
1 cup Mexican blend shredded cheese
1 ½ cups salsa
4 ea scallions, chopped

Procedure

Blend guacamole ingredients for 3-4 minutes until creamy.
In a serving bowl, layer the chips, lettuce, beans, cheese, salsa, and
scallions. Top with the guacamole and serve.

Yield: 8 cups

Nutrition Facts

Serving size: ¼ recipe

Amount Per Serving	
Calories	527.41
Calories From Fat (36%)	192.49
	% Daily Value
Total Fat 22.13g	34%
Saturated Fat 5.68g	28%
Cholesterol 16.92mg	6%
Sodium 1539.02mg	64%
Potassium 1352.52mg	39%
Total Carbohydrates 67.35g	22%
Fiber 15.81g	63%
Sugar 6.98g	
Protein 21.16g	42%

Baked Quorn Steaks

1 tsp olive oil	2 Tbsp chopped fresh basil
1 cup diced zucchini	1/4 tsp salt
1/2 cup minced onion	1/4 tsp ground black pepper
1 clove garlic peeled and minced	4 (6 oz) Quorn patties
2 cups diced fresh tomatoes	1/3 cup crumbled feta cheese

Procedure

1   Preheat oven to 400 degrees F (230 degrees C). Lightly grease a shallow baking dish.

2   Heat olive oil in a medium saucepan over medium heat and stir in zucchini, onion, and garlic. Cook and stir 5 minutes or until tender. Remove saucepan from heat and mix in tomatoes, basil, salt, and pepper.

3   Arrange Quorn in a single layer in the prepared baking dish. Spoon equal amounts of the zucchini mixture over each patty. Top with feta cheese.

4   Bake 15 minutes in the preheated oven.

Servings: 4

Yield: 4

Preparation Time: 15 minutes

Cooking Time: 15 minutes

Total Time: 30 minutes

Nutrition Facts

Serving size: 1/4 of a recipe (12.6 ounces).

Amount Per Serving	
Calories	344.39
Calories From Fat (41%)	141.09
	% Daily Value
Total Fat 15.78g	24%
Saturated Fat 3.93g	20%
Cholesterol 129.91mg	43%
Sodium 395.35mg	16%
Potassium 1022.78mg	29%
Total Carbohydrates 8.25g	3%
Fiber 2.63g	11%
Sugar 4.55g	
Protein 41.54g	83%

Recipe Type

Dinner

Blackened Quorn Steaks with Mango Salsa

2 Tbsp olive oil
2 Tbsp lime juice
2 Cloves garlic minced
4 Quorn patties
1 fresh mango peeled, pitted and chopped
1/4 cup finely chopped red bell pepper
1/2 Spanish onion, finely chopped
1 green onion chopped
2 Tbsp chopped fresh cilantro
1 Jalapeno pepper seeded and minced
2 Tbsp lime juice

1 1/2 tsp olive oil
2 Tbsp paprika
1 Tbsp cayenne pepper
1 Tbsp onion powder
2 tsp salt
1 tsp ground black pepper
1 tsp dried thyme
1 tsp dried basil
1 tsp dried oregano
1 Tbsp garlic powder
4 Tbsp olive oil

Procedure

1   Whisk together the olive oil, lime juice, and garlic in a bowl. Brush the Quorn with the olive oil and then rub the Quorn with the mixture.

2   Combine the mango, bell pepper, Spanish onion, green onion, cilantro, and jalapeno pepper in a bowl: stir. Add the lime juice and 1 1/2 teaspoons olive oil and toss to combine. Chill in refrigerator 1 hour.

3   Stir together the paprika, cayenne pepper, onion powder, salt, pepper, thyme, basil, oregano, and garlic powder in a bowl. Dip each side of each patty in the spice mixture to coat.

4   Heat 2 tablespoons olive oil in a large skillet over medium heat. Gently lay the patties into the hot oil. Cook the patty on one side for 4 minutes; remove to a plate. Pour the remaining 2 tablespoons olive oil into the skillet and let it get hot. Lay the patty with the uncooked side down into the skillet and cook another 4 minutes; remove from heat immediately.

5   Spoon about 1/2 cup of the mango salsa onto each of 4 plates. Lay the patties atop the salsa and serve immediately.

Servings: 4
Yield: 4
Preparation Time: 45 minutes
Cooking Time: 10 minutes
Total Time: 3 hours and 55 minutes

Nutrition Facts

Serving size:
1/4 of a recipe
(5.4 ounces).

Amount Per Serving	
Calories	298.08
Calories From Fat (71%)	212.04
	% Daily Value
Total Fat 24.02g	37%
Saturated Fat 3.51g	18%
Cholesterol 8.08mg	3%
Sodium 1180.88mg	49%
Potassium 382.67mg	11%
Total Carbohydrates 17.21g	6%
Fiber 3.89g	16%
Sugar 8.51g	
Protein 7.17g	14%

Recipe Type

Dinner

Vegetable Skewers with Rosemary-Dijon Vinaigrette

Skip the Quorn to make this vegan.

Rosemary-Dijon Vinaigrette

4 Tbsp sherry vinegar

4 Tbsp Grey Poupon Dijon mustard

3 Tbsp small shallots, minced

2 Tbsp lemon juice

1 Tbsp grated lemon zest

2/3 cup olive oil

2 Tbsp chopped fresh rosemary

Vegetable Skewers

2 Quorn patties

2 small red potatoes, quartered and cooked

24 sugar snap peas

24 button mushrooms

1 red bell pepper, cut into 1-inch pieces

1 red onion, cut into 1-inch pieces

1 medium yellow squash, cut into 12 rounds

1 medium zucchini, cut into 12 rounds

Procedure

To make Rosemary-Dijon Vinaigrette:

Combine all ingredients in a small bowl and whisk together.

To make Vegetable Skewers:

Cut Quorn into chunks. Thread vegetables and Quorn onto wooden skewers.

Place skewers into a baking dish.

Baste generously with the vinaigrette. Reserve ¼ of the vinaigrette.

Marinate overnight in the refrigerator.

Broil vegetables until just blackened, turning once.

Brush remaining vinaigrette over the vegetables. Yield: 6 servings

Nutrition Facts

Serving size: 1/6 recipe (about 18 oz)

Amount Per Serving	
Calories	580.45
Calories From Fat (39%)	229.07
	% Daily Value
Total Fat 26g	40%
Saturated Fat 3.61g	18%
Cholesterol 0.42mg	<1%
Sodium 154.05mg	6%
Potassium 1751.61mg	50%
Total Carbohydrates 72.77g	24%
Fiber 12.55g	50%
Sugar 6.52g	
Protein 21.25g	43%

Boneless Buffalo Wings

oil for deep frying
1 cup Pamela's Gluten-free baking mix
1/2 tsp ground black pepper
1/2 tsp cayenne pepper
1/4 tsp garlic powder
1/2 tsp paprika

1 egg
3/4 cup milk
1 Tablespoon olive oil
3 Quorn patties (slightly thawed), cut into 1/2" slices
1/4 cup hot pepper sauce
1 Tbsp butter

Procedure

1   Heat oil in a deep-fryer or large saucepan to 375 degrees F (190 degrees C).

2   Combine Pamela's baking mix, black pepper, cayenne pepper, garlic powder, and paprika in a large bowl. Whisk together the egg and milk in a small bowl. Dip each piece of Quorn in the egg mixture, and then roll in the flour blend. Repeat so that each piece of Quorn is double coated. Refrigerate breaded Quorn for 20 minutes.

3   Fry Quorn in the hot oil, in batches. Cook until the exterior is nicely browned, and the juices run clear, 5 to 6 minutes a batch.

4   Combine hot sauce and butter in a small bowl. Microwave sauce on high until melted, 20 to 30 seconds. Pour sauce over the cooked Quorn; mix to coat.

Servings: 3
Yield: 3
Preparation Time: 10 minutes
Cooking Time: 20 minutes
Total Time: 50 minutes

Nutrition Facts

Serving size: 1/3 of a recipe (10.8 ounces).

Amount Per Serving	
Calories	1060.15
Calories From Fat (72%)	763.34
	% Daily Value
Total Fat 86.3g	133%
Saturated Fat 11.93g	60%
Cholesterol 146.5mg	49%
Sodium 611.94mg	25%
Potassium 434.06mg	12%
Total Carbohydrates 36.07g	12%
Fiber 1.51g	6%
Sugar 3.61g	
Protein 35.44g	71%

Recipe Type

Dinner

Brazilian Black Bean Stew

Melissa's soyrizo can be found at many health food stores or on Amazon.com.

1 Tbsp olive oil
1/4 pound Melissa's soyrizo sausage, chopped
1 medium onion, chopped
2 clove garlic minced
2 (1 pound) sweet potatoes peeled and diced
1 large red bell pepper, diced
2 (14.5 oz) can diced tomatoes with juice

1 small hot green chile pepper diced
1 1/2 cup water
2 (16 oz) can black beans rinsed and drained
1 mango peeled, seeded and diced
1/4 cup chopped fresh cilantro
1/4 tsp salt

Procedure

1   Heat the oil in a large pot over medium heat, and cook the soyrizo 2 to 3 minutes. Place the onion in the pot, and cook until tender. Stir in garlic, and cook until tender, then mix in the sweet potatoes, bell pepper, tomatoes with juice, chile pepper, and water. Bring to a boil, reduce heat to low, cover, and simmer 15 minutes, until sweet potatoes are tender.

2   Stir the beans into the pot, and cook uncovered until heated through. Mix in the mango and cilantro, and season with salt.

Servings: 6
Yield: 6
Preparation Time: 15 minutes
Cooking Time: 30 minutes
Total Time: 45 minutes

Nutrition Facts

Serving size: 1/6 of a recipe (13.1 ounces).

Amount Per Serving	
Calories	309.87
Calories From Fat (30%)	92.62
	% Daily Value
Total Fat 10.27g	16%
Saturated Fat 3.03g	15%
Cholesterol 16.41mg	5%
Sodium 676.66mg	28%
Potassium 1150.91mg	33%
Total Carbohydrates 44.45g	15%
Fiber 8.16g	33%
Sugar 10.71g	
Protein 12.06g	24%

Recipe Type

Stew

Burrito Pie

1 pound Marjon vegetarian hamburger tofu crumbles
1 onion chopped
1 tsp minced garlic
6 Tbsp black olives, sliced
1/2 (4 oz) can diced green chili peppers

1/2 (10 oz) can diced tomatoes with habanero chili peppers
1 (16 oz) jar Taco Bell hot restaurant sauce
1 (16 oz) can refried beans
6 (8 inch) rice flour tortillas
4.5 oz shredded Colby cheese

Procedure

1 Preheat oven to 350 degrees F (175 degrees C).

2 In a large skillet over medium heat, sauté the Marjan crumbles for 5 minutes. Add the onion and garlic, and sauté for 5 more minutes. Mix in the olives, green chile peppers, tomatoes with green chile peppers, and taco sauce. Stir mixture thoroughly, reduce heat to low, and let simmer for 15 to 20 minutes.

3 Spread a thin layer of the meat mixture in the bottom of a 4 quart casserole dish. Cover with a layer of tortillas spread with refried beans, followed by more Marjan mixture, then a layer of cheese. Repeat tortilla/bean, meat, cheese pattern until all the tortillas are used, topping off with a layer of meat mixture and cheese.

4 Bake for 20 to 30 minutes in the preheated oven, or until cheese is slightly brown and bubbly.

Servings: 8
Yield: 1 pie
Preparation Time: 30 minutes
Cooking Time: 30 minutes
Total Time: 1 hour

Nutrition Facts

Serving size: 1/8 of a recipe (6.1 ounces).

Amount Per Serving	
Calories	283.83
Calories From Fat (44%)	124.41
	% Daily Value
Total Fat 13.69g	21%
Saturated Fat 5.22g	26%
Cholesterol 42.47mg	14%
Sodium 606.51mg	25%
Potassium 340.94mg	10%
Total Carbohydrates 20.99g	7%
Fiber 2.85g	11%
Sugar 2.11g	
Protein 18.37g	37%

Recipe Type

Pie

Curried Quorn Kabobs

For the Marinade:
1 tsp 3/4 cup canned coconut milk
1 (8 oz) can tomato sauce
1 garlic clove, minced
3 Tbsp curry powder
1 tsp ground black pepper
1 tsp ground cumin
1 tsp onion powder

For the Kabobs:
4 Quorn patties, cut into chunks
1 onion cut into wedges
12 cherry or grape tomatoes
12 mushrooms
1 bell pepper, seeded and cut into wedges

Procedure

1 In a small bowl, mix together all marinade ingredients.

2 Begin to assemble kabobs by placing vegetables and Quorn on skewers.

3 Soak kabobs in marinade for a minimum of 15 min, up to 1 day in the refrigerator.

4 When ready to cook kabobs, preheat the broiler or grill to medium high.

5 Cook for 10 min, turning and brushing with marinade as needed. Cook for 10 additional minutes and remove from heat. Serve immediately.

Servings: 4
Yield: 4
Preparation Time: 20 minutes
Cooking Time: 20 minutes

Nutrition Facts

Serving size: 1/4 of a recipe (17.4 ounces).

Amount Per Serving	
Calories	185.88
Calories From Fat (26%)	47.79
	% Daily Value
Total Fat 5.75g	9%
Saturated Fat 1g	5%
Cholesterol 0mg	0%
Sodium 352.66mg	15%
Potassium 1214.13mg	35%
Total Carbohydrates 26.03g	9%
Fiber 5.52g	22%
Sugar 6.58g	
Protein 13.09g	26%

Recipe Type

Barbecue, Dinner

Sesame Chik'n with Peanut Sauce

½ tsp olive oil
2 ¼ tsp toasted sesame oil
¼ cup finely chopped onion
3 green onions, minced
1 clove garlic, minced
2 Tbsp grated carrot
1 ½ cups Quorn patties, cut into 1" chunks
1 Tbsp Bragg's liquid aminos
1 ½ tsp vegan chicken broth
1 Tbsp floral honey
 Pinch cayenne pepper (optional)
8 large Romaine lettuce leaves
8 Tbsp San-J Thai peanut sauce

Procedure

Heat oils in a wok or large frying pan over medium heat.

Fry Quorn for 2-3 minutes until slightly brown. Add chopped onion, green onions, garlic, carrot, and sauté until the onion is tender, 3 to 4 minutes.

Stir in the remaining ingredients, except the lettuce and sauce, and stir fry for an additional 5 minutes.

Remove from the heat and allow to cool briefly before using.

Place ¼ cup on each lettuce leaf, drizzle with 1 Tbsp of peanut sauce.

Yield: 8 servings

Nutrition Facts

Serving size: 1/8 of a recipe (2.4 ounces).

Amount Per Serving	
Calories	100.43
Calories From Fat (58%)	58.16
	% Daily Value
Total Fat 6.85g	11%
Saturated Fat 1.2g	6%
Cholesterol 0mg	0%
Sodium 165.99mg	7%
Potassium 154.67mg	4%
Total Carbohydrates 6.76g	2%
Fiber 1.16g	5%
Sugar 2.95g	
Protein 4.54g	9%

Indian Stuffed Peppers

The slow cooker will do all of the work for you in this dish. All you have to do for dinner is slice the tops from the peppers, remove the seeds, fill with the filling, and bake.

1 cup chopped onion
2 tsp French's yellow mustard
1 tsp cumin seeds
1 tsp ground coriander
½ tsp salt
¼ tsp cayenne pepper
2 cups shredded green cabbage
1 cup diced sweet potato
2 cups cooked chickpeas
1 Tbsp minced fresh ginger
3 cloves garlic, minced (about 1 Tbs.)
¼ cup vegetable broth
¼ cup chopped cilantro
2 Tbsp chopped roasted cashews
4 large red bell peppers
3/4 cup plain yogurt
2 ½ Tbsp prepared mango chutney

Procedure

Place onion, yellow mustard, cumin seeds, coriander, salt, cayenne pepper, cabbage, potato, chickpeas, ginger, garlic, and vegetable broth in a slow cooker. Cook for 6 hours.

When done, stir in cilantro and cashews.

Slice tops off peppers and remove seeds. Fill with slow cooker filling and place caps on top.

Place peppers in a deep baking pan. Place ½" water in the pan and cover with foil.

Bake for 40 minutes at 375 degrees.

Combine yogurt and chutney. Drizzle over peppers to serve.

Servings: 4

Nutrition Facts

Serving size: ¼ recipe

Amount Per Serving	
Calories	337.31
Calories From Fat (14%)	48.8
	% Daily Value
Total Fat 5.57g	**9%**
Saturated Fat 1.17g	6%
Cholesterol 2.91mg	**<1%**
Sodium 979.53mg	**41%**
Potassium 956.91mg	**27%**
Total Carbohydrates 58.27g	**19%**
Fiber 12.88g	**52%**
Sugar 13.81g	
Protein 13.04g	**26%**

Egg fried rice

Think you can't eat fried rice again? Think again! My son swears this tastes better than the fried rice from our local Chinese restaurant. Make sure to use dark sesame oil for the best flavor.

4 cups Texmati Rice Select light brown rice
4 Tbsp sesame oil
2 Quorn patties, chopped into ¼ inch chunks
1 onion chopped
1 red pepper chopped
1 yellow pepper chopped
1 cup snow peas
1 cup peas
8 Tbsp Bragg's liquid aminos
2 eggs beaten

Procedure

1. Cook rice according to package directions
2. brown Quorn in a skillet over medium heat in sesame oil
3. add onion and cook 3-4 minutes until onions are softened
4. add remaining vegetables and stir fry 3 minutes
5. add rice and Bragg's. Stir fry until all ingredients are combined well -- no more than 1-2 minutes
6. Push rice to side of pan. Add eggs, scramble and then combine with rice.

Servings: 4
Yield: 4
Degree of Difficulty: Easy
Cooking Time: 15 minutes
Total Time: 15 minutes

Nutrition Facts

Serving size: 1/4 of a recipe (29 ounces).

Amount Per Serving	
Calories	896.95
Calories From Fat (23%)	204.36
	% Daily Value
Total Fat 22.3g	34%
Total Carbohydrates 99.09g	33%
Protein 70.96g	142%

Recipe Type

Breakfast

Recipe Tips

The key is to use dark brown sesame oil, which adds more flavor.

Quorn Noodle Casserole

4 Quorn patties
2 garlic cloves, minced
1/2 onion chopped
12 oz Seitenbacher Gluten-Free Golden Ribbon Gourmet Pasta
1 (10.75 oz) can cream of mushroom soup
1 jar white pasta sauce

12 oz frozen broccoli, chopped
1 tsp crushed red pepper flakes
1/2 tsp thyme
salt to taste
ground black pepper to taste
1 1/2 cup Glutino gluten free cheddar flavor crackers
2 Tbsp butter

Procedure

1   Cook pasta according to package directions. Drain. Microwave Quorn patties 2-3 minutes until heated throughout. Cut patties into small pieces, and mix with noodles.

2   Sauté onion and garlic in a skillet until translucent, about five minutes.

3   In a separate bowl, mix together mushroom soup, pasta sauce, red pepper, and thyme. Season with salt and pepper. Gently stir together all ingredients. Place in a 2 quart baking dish.

4   Melt butter in a saucepan. Add crumbled crackers and stir well Top casserole with the buttery crackers.

5   Bake at 350 degrees F (175 degrees C) for about 30 minutes, until heated through and browned on top.

Servings: 6
Yield: 6
Preparation Time: 30 minutes
Cooking Time: 30 minutes
Total Time: 1 hour

Nutrition Facts

Serving size: 1/6 of a recipe (11.7 ounces).

Amount Per Serving	
Calories	484.14
Calories From Fat (30%)	147.54
	% Daily Value
Total Fat 16.64g	26%
Saturated Fat 4.57g	23%
Cholesterol 113.09mg	38%
Sodium 727.98mg	30%
Potassium 598.43mg	17%
Total Carbohydrates 51.58g	17%
Fiber 3.59g	14%
Sugar 3.31g	
Protein 31.69g	63%

Slow-Cooker Quorn Tortilla Soup

2 Quorn patties, finely diced
1 (15 oz) can Rotel diced tomatoes with habanero
1 (10 oz) can enchilada sauce
1 medium onion chopped
1 (4 ounce) can chopped green chile peppers
2 cloves garlic minced
4 cups water
2 tsp Vogue cuisine vegetarian chicken soup & base
2 tsp cumin
1 tsp chili powder

1 tsp salt
1/4 tsp black pepper
1 bay leaf
1 (10 oz) package frozen corn
1 can (15 oz) black beans
1 Tbsp chopped cilantro
7 corn tortillas
 vegetable oil
1 cup cheese, grated Mexican
1 avocado diced

Procedure

1   Place Quorn patties, tomatoes, enchilada sauce, onion, green chilies, and garlic into a slow cooker. Pour in water and chicken broth, and season with cumin, chili powder, salt, pepper, and bay leaf. Stir in corn and cilantro. Cover, and cook on Low setting for 6 to 8 hours or on High setting for 3 to 4 hours.

2   Preheat oven to 400 degrees F (200 degrees C).

3   Lightly brush both sides of tortillas with oil. Cut tortillas into strips, and then spread on a baking sheet.

4   Bake in preheated oven until crisp, about 10 to 15 minutes. To serve, sprinkle cheese, tortilla strips and avocado over soup.

Servings: 8
Preparation Time: 30 minutes
Cooking Time: 8 hours
Total Time: 8 hours and 30 minutes

Nutrition Facts

Serving size: 1/8 of a recipe (18.3 ounces).

Amount Per Serving	
Calories	408.09
Calories From Fat (29%)	117.28
	% Daily Value
Total Fat 13.36g	21%
Saturated Fat 3.5g	18%
Cholesterol 104.14mg	35%
Sodium 1057.35mg	44%
Potassium 804.7mg	23%
Total Carbohydrates 26.9g	9%
Fiber 6.14g	25%
Sugar 2.96g	
Protein 45.34g	91%

Spicy Spaghetti

1 package Marjon vegetarian hamburger tofu crumbles
2 jalapenos
1 can (15 oz) crushed tomatoes
1 jar spaghetti sauce
1 Tbsp fresh oregano
1 Tbsp fresh thyme
1 16 oz package corn spaghetti

Procedure

1. Combine all ingredients except for spaghetti in a large saucepan.
2. Bring to a boil and then reduce heat to simmer.
3. Cover pan and simmer for 2 hours.
4. Remove jalapenos with 1 cup sauce and blend until jalapenos are well mixed.
5. Return jalapeno mix to pan and stir well.
6. Cook spaghetti according to package directions.

Servings: 4

Yield: 4

Nutrition Facts

Serving size: 1/4 of a recipe (10.9 ounces).

Amount Per Serving	
Calories	165.54
Calories From Fat (19%)	31.24
	% Daily Value
Total Fat 3.6g	6%
Saturated Fat 0.67g	3%
Cholesterol 1.29mg	<1%
Sodium 550.71mg	23%
Potassium 671.97mg	19%
Total Carbohydrates 29.3g	10%
Fiber 4.5g	18%
Sugar 10.85g	
Protein 7.22g	14%

Recipe Type

Pasta

Recipe Tips

If you can't find tofu crumbles, try Quorn crumbles or any vegetarian ground beef substitute.

Author Notes

Think tofu is tasteless? Think again! This recipe is loved by our entire family, who swear it must be ground beef.

Vegan Lunch

Vegetable Pakoras

These are a tasty addition to an Indian dish (such as a dal or curry). I use a Fry Daddy to fry veggies. With an old-fashioned pan, heat the oil to 375°. Note that the calories in this recipe account for the entire quart of oil. The actual fat content will be much less, depending on how much of the oil is left over from cooking. Still, this deep fried recipe isn't one if you're watching calories!

1 quart oil

1 cup besan

½ tsp ground coriander

¼ tsp salt

1 tsp ground turmeric

½ tsp chili powder

½ tsp garam masala

2 cloves garlic, minced

¾ cup water

4 cups vegetables: cauliflower, green beans, mushrooms, onion rings, slices of sweet potato, ¾" carrot chunks

Procedure

Warm oil to 375 degrees while preparing vegetables (if not already prepared)

In a large bowl, combine the besan, coriander, salt, turmeric, chili powder, garam masala, garlic, and water.

Mix well to form a smooth batter. Toss the vegetables into the batter and mix well, evenly coat vegetables.

Fry for 3-4 minutes until golden brown. Drain on paper towels before serving. Yield: 4 cups

Nutrition Facts

Serving size: 2/3 cup

Amount Per Serving	
Calories	1594.21
Calories From Fat (82%)	1302.77
	% Daily Value
Total Fat 147.47g	227%
Saturated Fat 14.98g	75%
Cholesterol 0mg	0%
Sodium 405.03mg	17%
Potassium 3129.41mg	89%
Total Carbohydrates 61.81g	21%
Fiber 26.51g	106%
Sugar 25.29g	
Protein 23.05g	46%

Vegan "Tuna" Salad

Not tuna...but you'll think it is!

3/4 cup raw sunflower seeds (soaked for 8 hours)

½ cup raw almonds (soak for 8 hours)

2 stalks celery chopped

1 clove garlic minced

1 Tbsp lemon juice

½ tsp dry dill weed

1/8 tsp celery seed

1-2 Tbsp olive oil

Procedure

Place all ingredients in the food processor with the S blade and process until the mixture resembles tuna salad.

Yield: 4 servings

Nutrition Facts

Serving size: ¼ recipe (about 2½ oz)

Amount Per Serving	
Calories	257.65
Calories From Fat (75%)	192.49
	% Daily Value
Total Fat 22.82g	35%
Saturated Fat 2.09g	10%
Cholesterol 0mg	0%
Sodium 21.07mg	<1%
Potassium 324.31mg	9%
Total Carbohydrates 9.16g	3%
Fiber 4.12g	16%
Sugar 1.66g	
Protein 8.23g	16%

Black Bean and Corn Salad

1 (15 oz) can black beans rinsed and drained
1 small yellow bell pepper chopped
1 small red bell pepper chopped
1 small tomato chopped
1 cup canned corn
2 scallions chopped
1 Tbsp chopped fresh cilantro

1 tsp dried oregano
1 tsp dried basil
1/2 tsp ground cumin
1/2 lime juice
  kosher or sea salt to taste
  Freshly ground black pepper to taste

Procedure

1   Combine all ingredients in a salad bowl. Let sit for 30 minutes in the fridge to allow flavors to blend. Serve chilled or at room temperature.

Servings: 4
Yield: 4
Preparation Time: 15 minutes

Nutrition Facts

Serving size: 1/4 of a recipe (5.8 ounces).

Amount Per Serving	
Calories	207.43
Calories From Fat (2%)	3.8
	% Daily Value
Total Fat 0.45g	<1%
Saturated Fat 0.09g	<1%
Cholesterol 0mg	0%
Sodium 217.04mg	9%
Potassium 402.85mg	12%
Total Carbohydrates 46.12g	15%
Fiber 4.25g	17%
Sugar 1.66g	
Protein 4.91g	10%

Recipe Type

Salad

Black Bean Cakes with Mango Salsa

For the Bean cake:

1/2 cup salsa
2 tsp ground cumin
2 (15 oz) can black beans , drained
1 1/2 cup Gluten free bread crumbs
1/4 cup finely chopped scallions
  kosher or sea salt to taste
  black pepper to taste
  vegetable oil cooking spray

For the Salsa:

2 mangoes, peeled and cubed
1/4 cup finely chopped red onion
1/4 cup finely chopped red bell
pepper
2 Tbsp finely chopped scallions
2 Tbsp finely chopped fresh cilantro
2 Tbsp fresh lime juice
2 tsp agave nectar
  pinch cayenne pepper

Procedure

1	Preheat the oven to 200 degrees F. Combine the salsa, cumin and black beans in a food processor and pulse until smooth. Add 1 cup bread crumbs, scallions, salt and black pepper.

2	Divide the mixture into 4 patties. Dredge the patties in the remaining 1/2 cup bread crumbs. Set the patties on a tray and refrigerate for 30 min.

3	While the bean cakes chill, combine all salsa ingredients and then chill.

4	Heat a non stick large skillet over medium heat. Using cooking spray throughout the sauté process, sauté the cake for about 3 min per side. Serve the cakes with the salsa.

Servings: 4
Yield: 4
Preparation Time: 30 minutes
Cooking Time: 30 minutes

Nutrition Facts

Serving size: 1/4 of a recipe (10.6 ounces).

Amount Per Serving	
Calories	368.91
Calories From Fat (8%)	30.59
	% Daily Value
Total Fat 3.53g	5%
Saturated Fat 0.76g	4%
Cholesterol 0mg	0%
Sodium 770.48mg	32%
Potassium 727.83mg	21%
Total Carbohydrates 72.27g	24%
Fiber 12.22g	49%
Sugar 20.35g	
Protein 14.96g	30%

Recipe Type

Cakes, Lunch

Chickpeas with Onion and Tomato

1/4 cup vegetable broth
1 medium onion chopped
3 plum tomatoes, chopped
2 cloves garlic, minced
1 bay leaf

1/2 tsp dried oregano
1 (15 oz) can chickpeas rinsed and
drained
kosher or sea salt to taste
Freshly ground black pepper to
taste

Procedure

1   Heat the broth in a skillet over medium high heat. Add onion and
cooked for 5 min. Put in the tomatoes and garlic and cook for 3 min.
Add the bay leaf and oregano. Lower heat, cover, and simmer for 15
min.

2   Put in the chickpeas, salt and black pepper, and cook for an
additional 5 min. or until chickpeas are heated through.

Servings: 6
Preparation Time: 10 minutes
Cooking Time: 25 minutes

Nutrition Facts

Serving size:
1/6 of a recipe
(4 ounces).

Amount Per Serving	
Calories	65.8
Calories From Fat (8%)	5.01
	% Daily Value
Total Fat 0.61g	<1%
Saturated Fat 0.06g	<1%
Cholesterol 0mg	0%
Sodium 193.97mg	8%
Potassium 189.28mg	5%
Total Carbohydrates 13.18g	4%
Fiber 2.6g	10%
Sugar 0.88g	
Protein 2.59g	5%

Recipe Type

Main Dish, Side Dish, Vegetables

French Country Stew

1 Tbsp olive oil
1 large onion chopped
2 garlic clove minced
3 cups peeled and cubed butternut
squash
4 cups vegetable broth
3 cups coarsely chopped green
cabbage

1 Tbsp chopped fresh thyme
1/4 tsp crushed red pepper
1 (16 oz) can white beans drained
and rinsed
1 cup canned diced tomatoes
 kosher or sea salt to taste
 Freshly ground black pepper to
taste

Procedure

1   Sauté the onion and garlic in the olive oil in a skillet over medium heat for 5 min. Add the squash, cabbage, broth, thyme, and crushed red pepper and bring to boil.

2   Lower heat, cover and simmer on medium low for about 30 min, or until the squash is tender.

3   Add the beans and tomatoes, cover and continue to simmer 10 min. Season with salt and black pepper.

Servings: 4
Yield: 4
Preparation Time: 10 minutes
Cooking Time: 45 minutes

Nutrition Facts

Serving size:
1/4 of a recipe
(20.2 ounces).

Amount Per Serving	
Calories	452.84
Calories From Fat (16%)	70.4
	% Daily Value
Total Fat 7.94g	12%
Saturated Fat 1.53g	8%
Cholesterol 2.46mg	<1%
Sodium 1808.57mg	75%
Potassium 1955.68mg	56%
Total Carbohydrates 79.57g	27%
Fiber 16.04g	64%
Sugar 7.48g	
Protein 20.68g	41%

Recipe Type

Stew

Barbecue Tofu Kabobs

For the Barbecue Sauce:
1 (8 oz) can tomato paste
1/2 cup agave nectar
1 tsp Wright's liquid smoke
1 tsp ground cinnamon
1 tsp ground allspice
2 clove garlic, minced

2 Tbsp Bragg's liquid aminos
  pinch cayenne pepper
For the kabobs:
1 pound extra firm tofu, pressed
  wooden skewers, soaked for 1
hour in warm water
  vegetable oil cooking spray

Procedure

1   Combine all the barbecue sauce ingredients in a small
saucepan. Bring to a boil over medium heat. Lower heat to simmer
and cook for 5 min., stirring regularly. Set aside.

2   Cut the tofu into equal-size slabs, about 3/4 inch thick. Using two
wooden skewers per tofu piece, skewer tofu, separating skewers
about 1/2 inch from each other.

3   Coat grill rack with cooking spray. Preheat gas grill to a medium-
high heat. When the grill is ready, add the tofu and grill for 1 min. Turn
the tofu and brush with more barbecue sauce. Cook for additional 1
min., until the tofu is browned.

Servings: 4
Yield: 4
Preparation Time: 5 minutes
Cooking Time: 10 minutes

Nutrition Facts

Serving size:
1/4 of a recipe
(7.5 ounces).

Amount Per Serving	
Calories	274.75
Calories From Fat (22%)	59.4
	% Daily Value
Total Fat 7.1g	11%
Saturated Fat 0.71g	4%
Cholesterol 0mg	0%
Sodium 364.44mg	15%
Potassium 617.01mg	18%
Total Carbohydrates 46.7g	16%
Fiber 2.81g	11%
Sugar 40.57g	
Protein 13.38g	27%

Recipe Type

Barbecue

Bean and Rice Burgers

2 Tbsp olive oil
1 small onion chopped
1 garlic clove minced
1 tsp chili powder
1/2 tsp ground cumin
1/4 tsp cayenne pepper
1 pinch sea salt
1 pinch black pepper
1 cup canned pinto beans, rinsed and mashed.

1 cup cooked brown basmati rice
3/4 cup gluten free bread crumbs
1/4 cup finely chopped fresh parsley
6 slices vegan cheddar cheese
  Vegetable oil cooking spray
6 whole Udi's hamburger buns
1 large tomato thinly sliced
6 lettuce leaves
2 tsp French's yellow mustard

Procedure

1   Heat the oil in a large skillet over medium heat. Add the onion and garlic and sauté for 4 min. Add the chili powder, cumin, cayenne, salt and black pepper.

2   Remove pan from heat. Add the beans, rice, bread crumbs and parsley and stir until combined. Form into 6 patties, place them on a plate, and place in the refrigerator for about 30 min.

3   Heat a large skillet, preferably cast iron, over medium heat and coat it with cooking spray. Spray with oil and cook for about 4 min per side, until brown and heated through. Place one slice of cheese on top of the burger during the last minute of cooking. Serve on buns with tomato, lettuce and mustard.

Servings: 6
Yield: 6
Preparation Time: 1 hour
Cooking Time: 10 minutes

Nutrition Facts

Serving size: 1/6 of a recipe (14.8 ounces).

Amount Per Serving	
Calories	363.48
Calories From Fat (29%)	105.63

	% Daily Value
Total Fat 12.11g	19%
Saturated Fat 6.49g	32%
Cholesterol 29.85mg	10%
Sodium 539.19mg	22%
Potassium 730.5mg	21%
Total Carbohydrates 48.48g	16%
Fiber 6.91g	28%
Sugar 3.99g	
Protein 16.98g	34%

Recipe Type

Lunch

Spinach, Beet and Orange Salad

For the Dressing:

1 lime, juiced

4 Tbsp rice vinegar

For the Salad:

2 Tbsp agave nectar

1/2 can beets (plain, unpickled)

2 tsp paprika

2 tsp fresh ginger, grated

6 cups baby spinach

1/2 tsp chili powder

2 mandarin oranges

Procedure

1   Put the vinegar, agave nectar, paprika, ginger, and chili powder into a saucepan and bring to a boil. Add lime juice. Let dressing cool.

2   Arrange spinach on a platter and top with beets and oranges. Drizzle dressing over the spinach salad.

Servings: 4

Preparation Time: 20 minutes

Cooking Time: 1 hour and 20 minutes

Nutrition Facts

Serving size: 1/4 of a recipe (16.3 ounces).

Amount Per Serving	
Calories	205.33
Calories From Fat (18%)	37.36
	% Daily Value
Total Fat 5.01g	8%
Saturated Fat 2.58g	13%
Cholesterol 18mg	6%
Sodium 237.54mg	10%
Potassium 1069.01mg	31%
Total Carbohydrates 44.03g	15%
Fiber 9.28g	37%
Sugar 21.83g	
Protein 10.41g	21%

Recipe Type

Salad

Vegetarian Lunch

Strawberry and Feta Salad

1 cup slivered almonds
2 cloves garlic -- minced
1 tsp Dijon mustard
1/4 cup raspberry vinegar
2 Tbsp balsamic vinegar

2 Tbsp agave nectar
1/2 cup olive oil
1 head romaine lettuce, torn
1 pint fresh strawberries, sliced
1 cup crumbled feta cheese

Procedure

1   In a skillet over medium-high heat, cook the almonds, stirring frequently, until lightly toasted. Remove from heat, and set aside.

2   Place the garlic, Dijon mustard, raspberry vinegar, balsamic vinegar, agave and olive oil in a blender and blend for 15 seconds.

3   In a large bowl, toss together the toasted almonds, romaine lettuce, strawberries, and feta cheese. Cover with the dressing mixture, and toss to serve.

Servings: 10
Preparation Time: 15 minutes
Total Time: 15 minutes

Nutrition Facts

Serving size: 1/10 of a recipe (6.9 ounces).

Amount Per Serving	
Calories	270.18
Calories From Fat (70%)	187.95
	% Daily Value
Total Fat 21.73g	33%
Saturated Fat 3.64g	18%
Cholesterol 13.35mg	4%
Sodium 181.57mg	8%
Potassium 403.25mg	12%
Total Carbohydrates 15.69g	5%
Fiber 4.48g	18%
Sugar 9.18g	
Protein 6.43g	13%

Recipe Type

Salad

Strawberry Spinach Salad

Edward & Sons makes two vegan Worcestershire sauces; only one is gluten free, so make sure you purchase the GF version.

2 Tbsp sesame seeds
1 Tbsp poppy seeds
1/2 cup agave nectar
1/2 cup olive oil
1/4 cup distilled white vinegar
1/4 tsp paprika
1/4 tsp Edward & Sons Organic
Vegan Gluten Free Worcestershire
Sauce

1 Tbsp minced onion
10 ounces fresh spinach rinsed, dried and torn into bite size pieces
1 quart strawberries clean, hulled and sliced
1/4 cup almonds, blanched and slivered
1 cup feta cheese

Procedure

1   In a medium bowl, whisk together the sesame seeds, poppy seeds, agave, olive oil, vinegar, paprika, Worcestershire sauce and onion. Cover, and chill for one hour.

2   In a large bowl, combine the spinach, strawberries and almonds. Pour dressing over salad, and toss. Refrigerate 10 to 15 minutes before serving.

Servings: 4
Yield: 4
Preparation Time: 10 minutes
Total Time: 1 hour and 10 minutes

Nutrition Facts

Serving size: 1/4 of a recipe (8.2 ounces).

Amount Per Serving	
Calories	555.19
Calories From Fat (68%)	375.26
	% Daily Value
Total Fat 43.02g	66%
Saturated Fat 10.14g	51%
Cholesterol 33.34mg	11%
Sodium 479.98mg	20%
Potassium 600.33mg	17%
Total Carbohydrates 36.78g	12%
Fiber 4.31g	17%
Sugar 29.29g	
Protein 10.66g	21%

Recipe Type

Salad

Snacks, Dips and Desserts

Vegan Snacks, Dips and Desserts

Steph's Salsa

2 large fresh tomatoes, whole and unpeeled

1 can Roma tomatoes, chopped

1 Tbsp canned green chilies

2 Tbsp diced red onion

3 Tbsp finely chopped fresh cilantro

¾ tsp salt

1 Tbsp lime juice

Procedure

Place all ingredients in a blender and blend for 30 seconds. Serve with tortilla chips.

Yield: 14 servings

Nutrition Facts

Serving size: 1/14 of a recipe (0.8 ounces).

Amount Per Serving	
Calories	4.81
Calories From Fat (10%)	0.47
	% Daily Value
Total Fat 0.06g	<1%
Saturated Fat 0.01g	<1%
Cholesterol 0mg	0%
Sodium 125.99mg	5%
Potassium 55.66mg	2%
Total Carbohydrates 1.04g	<1%
Fiber 0.33g	1%
Sugar 0.64g	
Protein 0.23g	<1%

Avocado Dip

Serve this dip with carrot chips and blue corn chips.

2 avocados - peeled, pitted and diced

1 can black beans, drained and rinsed

1 can whole kernel corn, drained

1 ea medium red onion, minced

1 beefsteak tomato, finely chopped

2 tbsp lime juice

1 tbsp chopped fresh cilantro

1 tbsp fresh lemon juice

½ tsp cumin

2 tbsp chili powder

1 pinch ground black pepper

1 pinch salt

Procedure

Place all ingredients into a food processor and pulse until just blended.

Yield: 12 servings

Nutrition Facts

Serving size: 1/12 recipe (3 oz)

Amount Per Serving	
Calories	91.16
Calories From Fat (45%)	40.96
	% Daily Value
Total Fat 4.88g	8%
Saturated Fat 0.69g	3%
Cholesterol 0mg	0%
Sodium 180.42mg	8%
Potassium 321.9mg	9%
Total Carbohydrates 11.31g	4%
Fiber 4.44g	18%
Sugar 1.56g	
Protein 2.73g	5%

Five Pepper Hummus

1 large green bell pepper, seeded and chopped

1 can garbanzo beans, drained, 15oz

4 fresh jalapeno peppers, seeded

½ tsp citric acid

½ tsp cumin

1 jar banana peppers, drained, 16oz

1 clove garlic

1 tbsp ground cayenne pepper

2 tbsp ground black pepper

¼ cup tahini

Procedure

Place all ingredients into a food processor. Process until blended.
Serve with carrot chips.

Yield: 16 servings

Nutrition Facts

Serving size: 1/16 recipe

Amount Per Serving	
Calories	48.85
Calories From Fat (37%)	17.85
	% Daily Value
Total Fat 2.13g	3%
Saturated Fat 0.3g	2%
Cholesterol 0mg	0%
Sodium 48.76mg	2%
Potassium 108.04mg	3%
Total Carbohydrates 6.53g	2%
Fiber 1.68g	7%
Sugar 0.38g	
Protein 1.8g	4%

Sweet Fruity Dip and Chips

2 kiwis, peeled and diced into ¼" cubes

2 Golden Delicious apples, peeled, diced into ¼" cubes

 8-oz raspberries, quartered

1 lb strawberries, diced into ¼" cubes

2 tbsp fructose

3 tbsp 100% fruit preserves

10 corn tortillas

  butter flavored cooking spray

1/3 cup fructose

2 tsp cinnamon

Procedure

Preheat oven to 425 degrees.

In a large bowl, thoroughly mix kiwis, Golden Delicious apples, raspberries, strawberries, 2T fructose and 100% fruit preserves.

Cover and place in the fridge.

Spray each tortilla with cooking spray. Keep in a stack.

Cut into wedges and place into a large Ziplock bag.

Pour fructose and cinnamon into the bag, shaking as you pour to evenly distribute. Close bag and shake well.

Bake for 10 minutes until lightly browned.

Allow to cool slightly. Serve with fruit.

Yield: 10 servings

Nutrition Facts

Serving size: 1/10 recipe (about 7 oz)

Amount Per Serving	
Calories	353.88
Calories From Fat (7%)	25.44
	% Daily Value
Total Fat 2.91g	4%
Saturated Fat 0.63g	3%
Cholesterol 0mg	0%
Sodium 206.84mg	9%
Potassium 229.49mg	7%
Total Carbohydrates 81.17g	27%
Fiber 3.97g	16%
Sugar 59.93g	
Protein 3.41g	7%

Vegetarian Snacks, Dips and Desserts

Spinach and Artichoke Dip

The best accompaniment for this dip would be raw corn chips from your local health food store. These can also be found online. An alternative would be to serve with a selection of dipping veggies.

1 can artichokes, chopped into ¼" chunks

1 cup cooked spinach, chopped into 1/4" pieces

1 cup Vegenaise

1 cup Parmesan cheese

½ tsp garlic clove, minced

½ tsp garlic powder

1 dash hot sauce

1 pinch pepper

1 pinch salt

Procedure

Add all ingredients to a large bowl. Mix well.

Yield: 10 servings

Nutrition Facts

Serving size: 1/10 recipe (about 2 oz)

Amount Per Serving	
Calories	121.51
Calories From Fat (74%)	90.23
	% Daily Value
Total Fat 10.2g	16%
Saturated Fat 2.56g	13%
Cholesterol 17.87mg	6%
Sodium 295.16mg	12%
Potassium 70.53mg	2%
Total Carbohydrates 3.6g	1%
Fiber 0.64g	3%
Sugar 0.14g	
Protein 4.32g	9%

Basil Pesto Spread

1 cup packed fresh basil leaves,
finely chopped
2 cloves garlic chopped
1 (12.3 oz) package firm low fat
silken tofu

1 pinch salt
1 pinch black pepper

Procedure

1   Place all ingredients in a food processor, and process until
smooth. Season with salt and black pepper.

Yield: 1 1/2 cups
Preparation Time: 5 minutes

Nutrition Facts

Serving size:
Entire recipe
(5.8 ounces).

Amount Per Serving	
Calories	209.84
Calories From Fat (15%)	31.04
	% Daily Value
Total Fat 3.66g	6%
Saturated Fat 1.68g	8%
Cholesterol 0mg	0%
Sodium 409.32mg	17%
Potassium 1981.82mg	57%
Total Carbohydrates 37.81g	13%
Fiber 27.48g	110%
Sugar 1.67g	
Protein 22.31g	45%

Recipe Type

Spread

Cheezy Popcorn

2 Tbsp vegetable oil   1 Tbsp nutritional yeast
1/2 cup popcorn kernel

Procedure

1   Heat oil in a large, covered pan over medium heat with 3
popcorn kernels. When first kernel pops, add the rest of the kernels.
Shake the pan gently as the kernels pop. When popping decreases to
a 2 or 3 second gap, remove from heat.

2   Transfer the popcorn to large bowl. Sprinkle with nutritional yeast
and toss to mix.

Servings: 4

Preparation Time: 5 minutes

Nutrition Facts

Serving size:
1/4 of a recipe
(0.4 ounces).

Amount Per Serving	
Calories	75.17
Calories From Fat (84%)	63.26
	% Daily Value
Total Fat 7.15g	11%
Saturated Fat 0.54g	3%
Cholesterol 0mg	0%
Sodium 0.25mg	<1%
Potassium 9.71mg	<1%
Total Carbohydrates 2.59g	<1%
Fiber 0.45g	2%
Sugar 0.03g	
Protein 0.39g	<1%

Recipe Type

Snack

Creamy Almond Fruit Smoothie

2 cups almond milk
1 1/2 cup fresh blue berries
1 large banana
1 drop almond essence

2 Tbsp flax seeds
1 Tbsp agave nectar

Procedure

1   Place all ingredients in a blender and blend until smooth.
Servings: 4

Yield: 4

Preparation Time: 5 minutes

Nutrition Facts

Serving size:
1/4 of a recipe
(7.7 ounces).

Amount Per Serving	
Calories	154.23
Calories From Fat (22%)	34.67
	% Daily Value
Total Fat 3.97g	6%
Saturated Fat 1.7g	9%
Cholesterol 9.76mg	3%
Sodium 59.33mg	2%
Potassium 361.51mg	10%
Total Carbohydrates 26.69g	9%
Fiber 3.02g	12%
Sugar 20.1g	
Protein 5.36g	11%

Recipe Type

Dessert, Snack

Tomatillo and Cilantro Salsa

This makes a wonderful dip. Serve with warm queso cheese and tortilla chips.

1 small red onion chopped
1 1/2 pound fresh tomatillos, husks removed, chopped
2 jalapeño pepper, stems and seeds removed, chopped

1 cup packed cilantro leaves and tender stems
1 lime juiced
1 tsp kosher salt

Procedure

1   Process all ingredients in a food processor until smooth.

Yield: 4 1/2 cups
Preparation Time: 5 minutes

Nutrition Facts

Serving size: Entire recipe (39 ounces).

Amount Per Serving	
Calories	346.65
Calories From Fat (18%)	63.38
	% Daily Value
Total Fat 7.54g	12%
Saturated Fat 0.98g	5%
Cholesterol 0mg	0%
Sodium 1939.27mg	81%
Potassium 2539.39mg	73%
Total Carbohydrates 69.84g	23%
Fiber 18.04g	72%
Sugar 44.77g	
Protein 10.43g	21%

Recipe Type

Dips, Snack

Guacamole

3 avocados peeled, pitted and
mashed
1 lime juiced
1 tsp salt
1/2 cup diced onion

3 Tbsp chopped fresh cilantro
2 roma (plum) tomatoes, diced
1 tsp minced garlic
1 pinch ground cayenne pepper
(optional)

Procedure

1   In a medium bowl, mash together the avocados, lime juice, and
salt. Mix in onion, cilantro, tomatoes, and garlic. Stir in cayenne
pepper. Refrigerate 1 hour for best flavor, or serve immediately.

Servings: 4

Yield: 4

Preparation Time: 10 minutes

Total Time: 10 minutes

Nutrition Facts

Serving size:
1/4 of a recipe
(8.7 ounces).

Amount Per Serving	
Calories	263.74
Calories From Fat (71%)	186.27
	% Daily Value
Total Fat 22.27g	34%
Saturated Fat 3.23g	16%
Cholesterol 0mg	0%
Sodium 596.95mg	25%
Potassium 934.57mg	27%
Total Carbohydrates 17.98g	6%
Fiber 11.32g	45%
Sugar 3.69g	
Protein 3.92g	8%

Recipe Type

Appetizer

Pickled Onions

1/2 cup pickling salt (do not
substitute regular table salt)
2 quarts water
1 1/2 pound pearl onions, peeled
and steamed until tender
2 Tbsp brown sugar
3 cups cider vinegar
1 tsp black peppercorns, crushed
roughly in a mortar and pestle

1/4 tsp ground allspice
1/4 tsp hot pepper flakes
1 bay leaf crumbled
2 Tbsp snipped fresh chives

Procedure

1   Dissolve 1/4 cup salt in 1 quart water in a glass bowl. Add the
onions. Weight them gently with a plate that fits inside the bowl (I used
a can on a saucer). Let them stand overnight

2   Drain and then peel the onions. Remove tips of onions (leave the
root end intact) with a sharp knife. Place back in the bowl. Make
another brine with the remaining 1/4 cup pickling salt and water, pour it
over the onions, and then weight them gently again. Let them stand for
2 days in the refrigerator.

3   Bring the sugar and vinegar to a boil in a saucepan. Stir to
dissolve and then let the liquid cool to room temperature.

4   Drain and rinse the onions well. In a 1- quart Mason jar, layer the
onions, peppercorns, allspice, pepper flakes, bay leaf and chives.
Cover them with the cooled, sweetened vinegar. Cover the jar.

5   Refrigerate the jar for at least 3 weeks before eating. They will
keep for up to six months.

Servings: 40
Yield: 1 quart

Nutrition Facts

Serving size:
1/40 of a
recipe (1.8
ounces).

Amount Per Serving	
Calories	2.93
Calories From Fat (2%)	0.05
	% Daily Value
Total Fat 0.01g	<1%
Saturated Fat 0g	0%
Cholesterol 0mg	0%
Sodium 1.65mg	<1%
Potassium 3.37mg	<1%
Total Carbohydrates 0.75g	<1%
Fiber 0.03g	<1%
Sugar 0.67g	
Protein 0.02g	<1%

Recipe Type

Appetizer

Spinach Dip

1 tbsp olive oil
1 small onion finely chopped
4 cloves garlic, minced
1 (10 oz) package frozen chopped
spinach, thawed
1 (12.3 oz) package firm low fat
silken tofu
1 Tbsp freshly squeezed lemon
juice

1 tsp ground coriander
1 1/2 tsp kosher salt
1/4 tsp freshly ground black pepper
 pinch cayenne pepper

Procedure

1   Saute onion and garlic in olive oil over medium heat in a skillet
for 5 minutes until lightly brown.
2   Place the spinach in a clean dish towel. Squeeze and twist the
dish towel to press out as much water as possible from the spinach.
3   Place the spinach, onions, and garlic in a food processor and
process until well chopped. Add the remaining ingredients and process
until smooth.

Yield: 2 1/2 cups
Preparation Time: 35 minutes

Nutrition Facts

Serving size:
Entire recipe
(12.2 ounces).

Amount Per Serving	
Calories	132.59
Calories From Fat (14%)	18
	% Daily Value
Total Fat 2.08g	3%
Saturated Fat 0.25g	1%
Cholesterol 0mg	0%
Sodium 3012.6mg	126%
Potassium 790.76mg	23%
Total Carbohydrates 20.44g	7%
Fiber 6.93g	28%
Sugar 4.88g	
Protein 12.83g	26%

Recipe Type

Dips

Vegetarian Snacks, Dips and Desserts

Chocolate Cherry Shake

1 cup frozen cherries   3/4 cup milk
1 bananas

Procedure

1   Put all ingredients into a blender and blend until smooth.

Servings: 4

Preparation Time: 5 minutes

Nutrition Facts

Serving size: 1/4 of a recipe (4 ounces).

Amount Per Serving	
Calories	66.96
Calories From Fat (15%)	10.35
	% Daily Value
Total Fat 1.17g	2%
Saturated Fat 0.65g	3%
Cholesterol 3.66mg	1%
Sodium 22.19mg	<1%
Potassium 217.71mg	6%
Total Carbohydrates 13.2g	4%
Fiber 1.39g	6%
Sugar 9.42g	
Protein 2.19g	4%

Recipe Type

Snack

Fruit Kabobs with Peach Cream Dip

1 cup purple seedless grapes
1 cup chopped fresh mango
2 oranges, peeled and chopped
1 apple, chopped

2 (6 oz) container peach flavored
yogurt, low fat
1 tsp vanilla extract
2 tsp ground cinnamon
Wooden skewers

Procedure

1 In a small bowl, mix the yogurt, vanilla and cinnamon.
2 Place fruit on each skewer and serve with yogurt dip.

Servings: 6
Preparation Time: 5 minutes

Nutrition Facts

Serving size:
1/6 of a recipe
(5.3 ounces).

Amount Per Serving	
Calories	67.51
Calories From Fat (3%)	2.09
	% Daily Value
Total Fat 0.24g	<1%
Saturated Fat 0.05g	<1%
Cholesterol 0mg	0%
Sodium 47.19mg	2%
Potassium 194.16mg	6%
Total Carbohydrates 14.57g	5%
Fiber 1.96g	8%
Sugar 11.7g	
Protein 2.45g	5%

Recipe Type

Dips, Snack

Vegan Soup

Curried Cauliflower Soup

This unusual dish has its roots in British and Indian cooking.

2 Tbsp olive oil

1 small onion, chopped

1 medium tart apple, such as Granny Smith, peeled,   cored, and coarsely chopped

1 Tbsp curry powder

1 clove garlic, sliced

1 head cauliflower, chopped into 1-inch pieces

4 cups low-sodium vegetable broth

1 tsp agave nectar

1 tsp rice wine vinegar

Procedure

Place all ingredients except for honey and vinegar into a crock pot.

Cook on low for 6 hours.

Blend ½ of the mixture in a blender and return to soup.

Stir in agave and vinegar just before serving. Yield: 6 servings

Nutrition Facts

Serving size: 1/6 recipe (8.2 oz)

Amount Per Serving	
Calories	180.12
Calories From Fat (36%)	64.01
	% Daily Value
Total Fat 7.28g	11%
Saturated Fat 1.25g	6%
Cholesterol 1.64mg	<1%
Sodium 1090.91mg	45%
Potassium 387.15mg	11%
Total Carbohydrates 25.6g	9%
Fiber 3.8g	15%
Sugar 4.65g	
Protein 4.75g	10%

Orange Black Bean Soup

2 tbsp olive oil
3 garlic cloves finely chopped
1 1/4 cup chopped red onions
1 tsp ground cumin
1 tsp dried oregano
2 (15 oz) can black beans, with liquid
2 cups vegetable broth
pinch crushed red pepper
1 bay leaf
1/2 cup pulp free orange juice
kosher or sea salt to taste
  Freshly ground black pepper to taste
1/4 cup chopped fresh cilantro

Procedure

1   Heat the olive oil in a large sauce pan over medium heat. Add the garlic, cumin, oregano and 1 cup of the onions and cook for 5 min.

2   Add the beans with their liquid, the remaining 2 cups of vegetable broth, crushed red pepper and the bay leaf. Bring the soup to a boil, lower the heat and simmer, uncovered for 20 min. stirring occasionally. Add the orange juice, salt and black pepper.

3   Remove the bay leaf. Puree half the bean mixture in a blender or food processor and add back to the soup. Serve each bowl garnished with cilantro and remaining red onions.

Servings: 5
Yield: 5
Preparation Time: 10 minutes
Cooking Time: 35 minutes

Nutrition Facts

Serving size: 1/5 of a recipe (8.8 ounces).

Amount Per Serving	
Calories	194.88
Calories From Fat (10%)	20.16
	% Daily Value
Total Fat 2.29g	4%
Saturated Fat 0.52g	3%
Cholesterol 1.11mg	<1%
Sodium 957.12mg	40%
Potassium 492.29mg	14%
Total Carbohydrates 35.3g	12%
Fiber 8.38g	34%
Sugar 2.8g	
Protein 9.5g	19%

Recipe Type

Soups

Chickpea and Vegetable Soup

5 cups vegetable broth
1/2 cup quick-cooking brown rice
1 (15 oz) can chickpeas rinsed and drained
1 medium carrot, chopped
1/2 cup small cauliflower florets

1 (15 oz) can tomatoes, chopped
2 tsp dried basil
1 tsp dried oregano
 kosher or sea salt to taste
 Freshly ground black pepper to taste

Procedure

1 Combine all ingredients in a large saucepan, bring to a boil.
2 Simmer for 20 min.

Servings: 6
Yield: 6
Preparation Time: 10 minutes
Cooking Time: 30 minutes

Nutrition Facts

Serving size: 1/6 of a recipe (11 ounces).

Amount Per Serving	
Calories	129.19
Calories From Fat (7%)	9.06
	% Daily Value
Total Fat 1.09g	2%
Saturated Fat 0.08g	<1%
Cholesterol 0mg	0%
Sodium 638.81mg	27%
Potassium 218.65mg	6%
Total Carbohydrates 28.35g	9%
Fiber 3.93g	16%
Sugar 3.28g	
Protein 3.69g	7%

Recipe Type

Soups

Chinese Mushroom Soup

1 oz dried wood ear mushrooms
4 dried shiitake mushrooms
12 dried tiger lily buds
2 cups hot water
1/3 oz bamboo fungus
3 Tbsp Bragg's liquid aminos
5 Tbsp rice vinegar
1/4 cup corn starch
1 (8 oz) firm tofu, cut into 1/4 inch
strips

1 quart vegetable broth
1/4 tsp crushed red pepper flakes
1/2 tsp ground black pepper
3/4 tsp ground white pepper
1/2 Tbsp chili oil
1/2 Tbsp sesame oil
1 green onion sliced
1 cup Chinese dried mushrooms

Procedure

1   In a small bowl, place wood mushrooms, shiitake mushrooms, and lily buds in 1 1/2 cups hot water. Soak 20 minutes, until rehydrated. Drain, reserving liquid. Trim stems from the mushrooms, and cut into thin strips. Cut the lily buds in half.

2   In a separate small bowl, soak bamboo fungus in 1/4 cup lightly salted hot water. Soak about 20 minutes, until rehydrated. Drain, and mince.

3   In a third small bowl, blend Bragg's, rice vinegar, and 1 tablespoon cornstarch. Place 1/2 the tofu strips into the mixture.

4   In a medium saucepan, mix the reserved mushroom and lily bud liquid with the vegetable broth. Bring to a boil, and stir in the wood mushrooms, shiitake mushrooms, and lily buds. Reduce heat, and simmer 3 to 5 minutes. Season with red pepper, black pepper, and white pepper.

5   In a small bowl, mix remaining cornstarch and remaining water. Stir into the broth mixture until thickened.

6   Mix Bragg's mixture and remaining tofu strips into the saucepan. Return to boil, and stir in the bamboo fungus, chili oil, and sesame oil. Garnish with green onion to serve.

Servings: 4
Yield: 4
Preparation Time: 45 minutes
Cooking Time: 15 minutes
Total Time: 1 hour

Nutrition Facts

Serving size:
1/4 of a recipe
(27.1 ounces).

Amount Per Serving	
Calories	251.45
Calories From Fat (22%)	54.65
	% Daily Value
Total Fat 6.93g	11%
Saturated Fat 1.26g	6%
Cholesterol 2.46mg	<1%
Sodium 2034.62mg	85%
Potassium 643.03mg	18%
Total Carbohydrates 46.48g	15%
Fiber 4.15g	17%
Sugar 0.49g	
Protein 9.33g	19%

Recipe Type

Soups

Lentil Soup

2 tbsp olive oil	1 (14.5 oz) can crushed tomatoes
1 onion chopped	2 cups dry lentils, rinsed
2 carrots, diced	8 cups water
2 Stalks celery chopped	1/2 cup spinach rinsed and finely
2 cloves garlic clove, minced	chopped
1 tsp dried oregano	2 Tbsp cider vinegar
1 bay leaf	salt to taste
1 tsp dried basil	ground black pepper to taste

Procedure

1   In a large soup pot, heat oil over medium heat. Add onions, carrots, and celery; cook and stir until onion is tender. Stir in garlic, bay leaf, oregano, and basil; cook for 2 minutes.

2   Stir in lentils, and add water and tomatoes. Bring to a boil. Reduce heat, and simmer for at least 1 hour. When ready to serve stir in spinach, and cook until it wilts. Stir in vinegar, and season to taste with salt and pepper, and more vinegar if desired.

Servings: 6
Yield: 6

Nutrition Facts

Serving size: 1/6 of a recipe (18.6 ounces).

Amount Per Serving	
Calories	342.7
Calories From Fat (26%)	87.53
	% Daily Value
Total Fat 9.92g	15%
Saturated Fat 1.39g	7%
Cholesterol 0mg	0%
Sodium 190.42mg	8%
Potassium 927.97mg	27%
Total Carbohydrates 47.13g	16%
Fiber 21.83g	87%
Sugar 5.33g	
Protein 17.83g	36%

Recipe Type

Soups

Vegetarian Soup

Pasta Fagioli

3 Tbsp olive oil
1 onion quartered and halved
2 cloves garlic minced
1 (29 oz) can tomato sauce
5 1/2 cup water
1 Tbsp dried parsley
1 1/2 tsp dried basil
1 1/2 tsp dried oregano
1 tsp salt
1 (15 oz) can cannellini beans
1 (15 oz) can navy beans
1/3 cup grated Parmesan cheese
1/2 pound Bionaturae Organic Penne Rigate

Procedure

1   In a large pot over medium heat, cook onion in olive oil until translucent. Stir in garlic and cook until tender. Reduce heat, and stir in tomato sauce, water, parsley, basil, oregano, salt, cannelini beans, navy beans and Parmesan. Simmer 1 hour.

2   Bring a large pot of lightly salted water to a boil. Add pasta and cook for 8 to 10 minutes or until al dente; drain. Stir into soup.

Servings: 8
Yield: 8
Preparation Time: 10 minutes
Cooking Time: 1 hour and 30 minutes
Total Time: 1 hour and 40 minutes

Nutrition Facts

Serving size: 1/8 of a recipe (11.6 ounces).

Amount Per Serving	
Calories	250.5
Calories From Fat (24%)	61.19
	% Daily Value
Total Fat 6.96g	11%
Saturated Fat 1.54g	8%
Cholesterol 3.66mg	1%
Sodium 526.41mg	22%
Potassium 908.05mg	26%
Total Carbohydrates 34.85g	12%
Fiber 11.15g	45%
Sugar 3.02g	
Protein 14.02g	28%

Recipe Type

Soups

African Peanut Soup

1 tablespoon olive oil
1 Quorn chicken patty
1/2 onion chopped
1 red bell pepper, sliced
2 Clove garlic -- minced
1 14 ounce crushed tomatoes
1 sweet potato peeled and cut into bite size pieces
1 1/2 cups sliced carrots
8 tsp Vogue instant vegetarian chicken base dissolved in8 cups water

1/2 teaspoon curry powder
1/2 teaspoon ground cumin
1/4 teaspoon chili powder
1/4 teaspoon cayenne pepper
1/4 teaspoon crushed red pepper flakes
1/4 teaspoon ground cinnamon
1/4 teaspoon ground black pepper
1/2 cup brown rice
1/2 cup crunchy peanut butter

Procedure

1   Heat olive oil in a skillet over medium heat, and brown the Quorn breasts on both sides, about 2 minutes per side. Chop finely and place the Quorn into a slow cooker. Cook the onion, red bell peppers, and garlic in the hot skillet until the onions are translucent, about 5 minutes; transfer the cooked vegetables into the slow cooker.

2   Stir the crushed tomatoes, sweet potatoes, carrots, chicken broth, curry powder, cumin, chili powder, cayenne pepper, red pepper flakes, cinnamon, and black pepper into the slow cooker. Set the cooker to High, and cook for 5 to 6 hours, or cook on Low for 10 hours. Stir in additional chicken broth throughout the cooking time if needed.

3   Mix in the brown rice 3 hours before serving, and mix in the peanut butter at least 1 hour before serving.

Servings: 20
Yield: 20
Preparation Time: 30 minutes
Cooking Time: 5 hours
Total Time: 5 hours and 30 minutes

Nutrition Facts

Serving size: 1/20 of a recipe (3.5 ounces).

Amount Per Serving	
Calories	202
Calories From Fat (35%)	16.31
	% Daily Value
Total Fat 8.6g	13%
Saturated Fat 1.4g	7%
Cholesterol 13mg	4%
Sodium 161mg	7%
Potassium 502mg	14%
Total Carbohydrates 22.6g	8%
Fiber 4g	16%
Sugar 4.3g	
Protein 10.6g	21%

Fast Black Bean Soup

This recipe can be made vegan if you use vegan sour cream.

2 (15 oz) can black beans, drained and rinsed
1 1/2 cup vegetable broth
1 cup salsa

1 tsp ground cumin
4 Tbsp sour cream
2 Tbsp thinly sliced green onion

Procedure

1. In a food processor or blender, combine beans, broth, salsa, and cumin. Blend until fairly smooth.
2. Heat the bean mixture in a saucepan over medium heat until thoroughly heated.
3. Ladle soup into 4 individual bowls, and top each bowl with 1 tablespoon of the sour cream and 1/2 tablespoon green onion.

Servings: 4
Yield: 4
Preparation Time: 10 minutes
Cooking Time: 10 minutes
Total Time: 20 minutes

Nutrition Facts

Serving size: 1/4 of a recipe (9.1 ounces).

Amount Per Serving	
Calories	218.02
Calories From Fat (18%)	39.42
	% Daily Value
Total Fat 4.49g	7%
Saturated Fat 1.86g	9%
Cholesterol 7.16mg	2%
Sodium 1213.07mg	51%
Potassium 677.37mg	19%
Total Carbohydrates 35.12g	12%
Fiber 9.85g	39%
Sugar 2.49g	
Protein 11.25g	22%

Recipe Type

Soups

Squash and Sweet Potato Soup

2 Tbsp unsalted butter
1 cup diced onion
6 cups butternut squash peeled, seeded and cut into 1-inch cubes
4 cups sweet potatoes peeled and cut into 1-inch cubes
6 cups reduced-sodium vegetable broth
3 Tbsp chopped fresh thyme

1 Tbsp grated fresh ginger root
1 tsp ground turmeric
1/2 tsp ground coriander
1/4 tsp ground black pepper
1 green chili peppers, halved lengthwise (optional)
1 cup silken tofu, divided
salt to taste

Procedure

1   Melt the butter in a large stock pot over medium heat. Stir in the onion; cook and stir until the onion has softened and turned translucent, about 5 minutes. Add the butternut squash, sweet potatoes, and enough vegetable broth to cover. Stir in the thyme, ginger, turmeric, coriander, black pepper, and chile pepper. Bring to a boil over medium-high heat, then reduce heat to medium-low. Cover and simmer until vegetables are very tender, 20 to 30 minutes, stirring occasionally.

2   Pour about 1/3 of the soup and 1/3 of the tofu into a blender. Puree in batches until smooth.

Servings: 6
Yield: 6
Preparation Time: 35 minutes
Cooking Time: 30 minutes
Total Time: 1 hour and 5 minutes

Nutrition Facts

Serving size: 1/6 of a recipe (17.5 ounces).

Amount Per Serving	
Calories	322.88
Calories From Fat (23%)	73.18
	% Daily Value
Total Fat 8.27g	13%
Saturated Fat 3.43g	17%
Cholesterol 12.64mg	4%
Sodium 1789.83mg	75%
Potassium 1131.83mg	32%
Total Carbohydrates 55.9g	19%
Fiber 8.43g	34%
Sugar 6.19g	
Protein 9.68g	19%

Recipe Type

Soups

Cauliflower Potato Chowder

2 tbsp olive oil
4 large shallots, minced
1/2 cup chopped celery
3 cups vegetable broth
6 cups cauliflower florets (about 1 medium head)
1 cup chopped red bell pepper
1 medium potato, peeled and cut into 1/2 inch cubes (about 1 1/2 cups)

1 bay leaf
1 cup 2% milk
2 Tbsp finely chopped fresh basil
kosher salt to taste
freshly ground black pepper to taste

Procedure

1 Heat olive oil in a large sauce pan over medium heat. Add the shallots and celery and sauté for 5min. Add the remaining 3 cups broth and 1 cup water and bring to boil. Add the cauliflower, bell pepper, sweet potato and bay leaf and bring to a boil.

2 Reduce the heat, cover and simmer for 20 min. Remove the bay leaf.

3 Add the milk. puree half the soup in a blender and then combine with the unblended soup. Add the basil and season with salt and black pepper.

Servings: 6
Yield: 6
Preparation Time: 20 minutes
Cooking Time: 35 minutes

Nutrition Facts

Serving size: 1/6 of a recipe (11.6 ounces).

Amount Per Serving	
Calories	167.39
Calories From Fat (18%)	29.39
	% Daily Value
Total Fat 3.31g	5%
Saturated Fat 1.1g	6%
Cholesterol 4.59mg	2%
Sodium 999.67mg	42%
Potassium 761.79mg	22%
Total Carbohydrates 28.8g	10%
Fiber 5.48g	22%
Sugar 5.75g	
Protein 7.58g	15%

Recipe Type

Soups

Cream of Asparagus

3 cups sliced asparagus
2 cups vegetable broth
3/4 tsp chopped fresh thyme
1 bay leaf
1 garlic clove, crushed
2 Tbsp rice flour
2 cups milk

pinch ground nutmeg
1 tsp salt
1/4 tsp grated lemon zest
1/2 Tbsp lemon juice
Freshly ground black pepper to taste
hot sauce to taste

Procedure

1   Combine asparagus, broth, 1/2 tsp thyme, bay leaf and garlic in a large saucepan over medium high heat. Bring to a boil. Cover, reduce heat, and simmer for 10 min. Discard the bay leaf. Place the mixture in a blender and puree until smooth.

2   Place the rice flour in a large sauce pan over medium heat. Gradually add the milk, stirring with a whisk until blended. Add the pureed asparagus mixture and nutmeg and stir to combine. Bring to a boil. Reduced heat and simmer for 5 min. Remove from heat and strain. Add the remaining 1/4 tsp thyme, salt, lemon juice, lemon zest and black pepper. Add hot sauce

Servings: 4
Yield: 4
Preparation Time: 5 minutes
Cooking Time: 35 minutes

Nutrition Facts

Serving size:
1/4 of a recipe
(19.9 ounces).

Amount Per Serving	
Calories	180.13
Calories From Fat (18%)	31.56
	% Daily Value
Total Fat 3.61g	6%
Saturated Fat 0.61g	3%
Cholesterol 1.23mg	<1%
Sodium 2462.98mg	103%
Potassium 902.66mg	26%
Total Carbohydrates 28.41g	9%
Fiber 5.72g	23%
Sugar 3.17g	
Protein 12.32g	25%

Recipe Type

Soups

Mulligatawny Soup

1/2 cup chopped onion
2 stalks celery chopped
1 carrot diced
1/4 cup butter
1 1/2 Tbsp rice flour
1 1/2 tsp curry powder
4 cups water
4 tsp Vogue Cuisine Vegetarian
Chicken Soup & Seasoning Base

1/2 apple cored and chopped
1/4 cup white rice uncooked
1 Quorn patty cut into tiny cubes
 salt to taste
 Ground black pepper to taste
1 pinch dried thyme
1/2 cup heavy cream, heated

Procedure

1 Sauté onions, celery, carrot, and butter in a large soup pot. Add flour and curry, and cook 5 more minutes. Add chicken stock, mix well, and bring to a boil. Simmer about 1/2 hour.

2 Add apple, rice, Quorn, salt, pepper, and thyme. Simmer 15-20 minutes, or until rice is done.

3 When serving, add hot cream and stir.

Servings: 6
Yield: 6
Preparation Time: 20 minutes
Cooking Time: 1 hour
Total Time: 1 hour

Nutrition Facts

Serving size: 1/6 of a recipe (15 ounces).

Amount Per Serving	
Calories	242.02
Calories From Fat (61%)	147.29
	% Daily Value
Total Fat 16.67g	26%
Saturated Fat 9.88g	49%
Cholesterol 59.69mg	20%
Sodium 584.65mg	24%
Potassium 327.62mg	9%
Total Carbohydrates 13.79g	5%
Fiber 1.48g	6%
Sugar 3.19g	
Protein 9.4g	19%

Recipe Type

Soups

Cheesy Potato Soup

2 cups water
2 cups peeled and cubed red potatoes
3 Tbsp melted butter
1 small onion chopped
3 Tbsp rice flour

salt and pepper to taste
3 cups milk
1/2 tsp agave nectar
1 cup shredded Cheddar cheese

Procedure

1 Using a medium sized stock pot bring water to a boil, add potatoes and cook until tender. Drain reserving 1 cup liquid.

2 Stir in butter, onion and flour. Season with salt and pepper. Gradually stir in potatoes, reserved liquid, milk, agave, and cheese. Simmer for 30 minutes, stirring frequently.

Servings: 10
Yield: 10

Nutrition Facts

Serving size: 1/10 of a recipe (6.9 ounces).

Amount Per Serving	
Calories	161.16
Calories From Fat (49%)	78.86
	% Daily Value
Total Fat 8.95g	14%
Saturated Fat 5.57g	28%
Cholesterol 26.88mg	9%
Sodium 133.41mg	6%
Potassium 259.6mg	7%
Total Carbohydrates 14.2g	5%
Fiber 0.86g	3%
Sugar 4.6g	
Protein 6.52g	13%

Recipe Type

Soups

Creamy Tomato Basil Soup

4 tomatoes peeled, seeded and diced
4 cups tomato juice
14 leaves fresh basil
1/2 cup milk

1/2 cup heavy whipping cream
1/2 cup butter
 salt and pepper to taste

Procedure

1   Place tomatoes and juice in a stock pot over medium heat. Simmer for 30 minutes. Add the basil leaves and puree with a hand blender.

2   Stir in the milk, cream and butter. Season with salt and pepper. Heat, stirring until the butter is melted. Do not boil.

Servings: 4
Yield: 4
Preparation Time: 10 minutes
Cooking Time: 35 minutes
Total Time: 45 minutes

Nutrition Facts

Serving size: 1/4 of a recipe (17.7 ounces).

Amount Per Serving	
Calories	428.41
Calories From Fat (73%)	313.54
	% Daily Value
Total Fat 35.7g	55%
Saturated Fat 22.21g	111%
Cholesterol 104.2mg	35%
Sodium 115.22mg	5%
Potassium 1393.06mg	40%
Total Carbohydrates 26.51g	9%
Fiber 8.75g	35%
Sugar 14.87g	
Protein 8.68g	17%

Recipe Type

Soups

Southwest Soup

1 cup mixed chopped peppers
1 can (15 oz) chopped tomatoes
1 can (15 oz) black beans
2 cups water
1 tsp vegetable bouillon
1/8 tsp black pepper
1/8 tsp cayenne pepper

1 Tbsp chili powder
1/4 tsp garlic powder
1/4 tsp salt
1/4 tsp oregano
1 pinch cumin seeds
2 Quorn patties, finely chopped

Procedure

1 Combine ingredients in a slow cooker and cook for 4 hours on "High."

Servings: 8
Yield: 8

Nutrition Facts

Serving size:
1/8 of a recipe
(10.5 ounces).

Amount Per Serving	
Calories	153.62
Calories From Fat (13%)	19.78
	% Daily Value
Total Fat 2.26g	3%
Saturated Fat 0.47g	2%
Cholesterol 37.78mg	13%
Sodium 391.63mg	16%
Potassium 627.8mg	18%
Total Carbohydrates 17.55g	6%
Fiber 5.55g	22%
Sugar 2.44g	
Protein 17.31g	35%

Recipe Type

Soups

Author Notes

Our family favorite. An easy slow-cooker recipe.

Vegetarian Tortilla Soup

2 Tbsp vegetable oil
1 pound package frozen pepper and onion stir fry mix
2 garlic clove, minced
3 Tbsp ground cumin
1 can (2 cups) crushed tomatoes with chili peppers
3 cans (4 ounce ea.) chopped green chile peppers, drained
4 cans (14 ounce ea.) vegetable broth

Salt and pepper to taste
1 can 11-oz whole kernel corn
12 ounces tortilla chips
1 cup shredded Cheddar cheese
1 avocado peeled, pitted and diced

Procedure

1   Heat the oil in a large pot over medium heat. Stir in the pepper and onion stir fry mix, garlic, and cumin, and cook 5 minutes, until vegetables are tender. Mix in the tomatoes and chile peppers. Pour in the broth, and season with salt and pepper. Bring to a boil, reduce heat to low, and simmer 30 minutes.

Servings: 12
Yield: 12
Preparation Time: 15 minutes
Cooking Time: 40 minutes
Total Time: 55 minutes

Nutrition Facts

Serving size: 1/12 of a recipe (2 ounces).

Amount Per Serving	
Calories	315
Calories From Fat (44%)	139.43
	% Daily Value
Total Fat 16.2g	25%
Saturated Fat 4g	20%
Cholesterol 12mg	4%
Sodium 1152mg	48%
Potassium 461mg	13%
Total Carbohydrates 37.2g	12%
Fiber 5.9g	24%
Sugar 3.9g	
Protein 8.7g	17%

Recipe Type

Soups

Vegan Salads

Green Pepper Tomato Salad

This tangy salad can be served as a side dish. Serve on a bed of lettuce for a full meal.

3 medium tomatoes, seeded and chopped

1 medium green pepper, chopped

1 celery rib, thinly sliced

1 cup chick peas, drained and rinsed

½ cup chopped red onion

2 tbsp cider vinegar

1 tbsp fructose

½ tsp salt

1/8 tsp pepper

Procedure

Combine first five ingredients in a bowl.

Mix last four ingredients in a small bowl.

Combine all ingredients. Chill in refrigerator for 1 hour before serving.

Yield: 6 servings

Nutrition Facts

Serving size: 1/6 recipe (about 6 oz)

Amount Per Serving	
Calories	79.64
Calories From Fat (7%)	5.62
	% Daily Value
Total Fat 0.67g	1%
Saturated Fat 0.09g	<1%
Cholesterol 0mg	0%
Sodium 324.12mg	14%
Potassium 295.01mg	8%
Total Carbohydrates 16.24g	5%
Fiber 3.33g	13%
Sugar 4.61g	
Protein 2.98g	6%

Pomegranate and Pine Nuts Salad

½ cup cashews, roasted

3 tbsp pine nuts

2 cups baby spinach

5 cups romaine lettuce, torn

1 ea garlic clove, thinly sliced

½ tbsp olive oil

½ avocado, cored

¼ cup Pomegranate seeds

2 tbsp Lemon juice

1 pinch salt

Procedure

Combine all ingredients in a large bowl and toss well.

Yield: 4 servings

Nutrition Facts

Serving size: ¼ recipe (about 5 oz)

Amount Per Serving	
Calories	214.28
Calories From Fat (69%)	147.71
	% Daily Value
Total Fat 17.55g	27%
Saturated Fat 2.59g	13%
Cholesterol 0mg	0%
Sodium 66mg	3%
Potassium 476.61mg	14%
Total Carbohydrates 12.83g	4%
Fiber 3.62g	14%
Sugar 3g	
Protein 5.23g	10%

Mexican Salad

1 can black beans

1 medium cucumber, chopped

1 can whole kernel corn, drained

4 ea Roma tomatoes, chopped

1 green bell pepper, chopped

1 red bell pepper, chopped

2 tbsp red wine vinegar

1 tbsp crushed red pepper flakes

½ tsp garlic, minced

½ tsp cumin

¼ tsp dried cilantro

¼ tsp salt

1/8 tsp ground black pepper

Procedure

Combine all ingredients in a bowl and mix well.

Cover, and chill at least 1 hour before serving. Yield: 6 servings

Nutrition Facts

Serving size: 1/6 recipe

Amount Per Serving	
Calories	101.65
Calories From Fat (7%)	6.94
	% Daily Value
Total Fat 0.82g	1%
Saturated Fat 0.12g	<1%
Cholesterol 0mg	0%
Sodium 241.32mg	10%
Potassium 620.47mg	18%
Total Carbohydrates 20.51g	7%
Fiber 5.91g	24%
Sugar 6.31g	
Protein 5.1g	10%

Chickpea Salad

1 can chickpeas, drained
1 ½ cups celery, diced
½ cup Vegenaise
2 Tbsp lemon juice
4 ea Roma tomatoes
2 Tbsp parsley
1 tsp garlic powder
1 tsp onion powder
 Salt and pepper, to taste
½   box   Glutino cheddar flavor crackers

Procedure

Combine all ingredients, except for crackers. Chill for at least 30 minutes before serving.

Serve with gluten free crackers.

Yield: 8 servings

Nutrition Facts

Serving size: 1/8 recipe (about 6 oz)

Amount Per Serving	
Calories	183.88
Calories From Fat (28%)	51.89
	% Daily Value
Total Fat 5.92g	9%
Saturated Fat 0.71g	4%
Cholesterol 5.67mg	2%
Sodium 397.55mg	17%
Potassium 328.51mg	9%
Total Carbohydrates 29.45g	10%
Fiber 4.88g	20%
Sugar 2.58g	
Protein 5.45g	11%

Fruit and Nut Salad

1 cup slivered almonds

6 teaspoons agave nectar

½ cup olive oil

¼ cup distilled white vinegar

1 pinch salt and pepper, each

½ head iceberg lettuce, chopped

½ head romaine lettuce, chopped

1 cup chopped celery

¼ cup chopped fresh chives

½ cup dried cranberries

¼ cup mandarin orange segments, drained

¼ cup sliced fresh peaches

¼ cup chopped fresh strawberries

Procedure

Combine almonds and 4 tsp agave in a frying pan. Cook over medium heat until almonds are coated. Remove almonds with a slotted spoon. Mix the olive oil, vinegar, 2 tsp agave, salt, and pepper in a small bowl. Mix all ingredients together in a large bowl. Toss well and serve.

Yield: 8 servings

Nutrition Facts

Serving size: 1/8 recipe (about 5 oz)

Amount Per Serving	
Calories	395.47
Calories From Fat (51%)	201.34
	% Daily Value
Total Fat 23.3g	36%
Saturated Fat 2.58g	13%
Cholesterol 0mg	0%
Sodium 57.34mg	2%
Potassium 272.39mg	8%
Total Carbohydrates 45.32g	15%
Fiber 5.28g	21%
Sugar 11.04g	
Protein 4.42g	9%

Cucumber Dill Salad

2 cups ½-inch cucumber cubes
1 cup ½-inch tomato pieces
¼ cup ¼-inch red onion pieces
½ tsp dried dill weed
⅛ tsp salt
⅛ tsp garlic powder
½ cup vegan sour cream

Procedure

Stir the celery seed, dill weed, salt, garlic powder and sour cream together. Add vegetables and toss.

Yield: 7 Servings

Nutrition Facts

Serving size: 1/7 of a recipe (2.3 oz).

Amount Per Serving	
Calories	11.06
Calories From Fat (10%)	1.08
	% Daily Value
Total Fat 0.13g	<1%
Saturated Fat 0.01g	<1%
Cholesterol 0mg	0%
Sodium 43.85mg	2%
Potassium 109.58mg	3%
Total Carbohydrates 2.26g	<1%
Fiber 0.65g	3%
Sugar 1.15g	
Protein 0.51g	1%

Black Bean-Avocado Salad

2 tbsp lemon juice

1 tbsp whole-grain mustard

1/8 tsp black pepper

1 pinch salt

2 tbsp olive oil

2 ea Roma tomatoes, chopped

1 can canned black beans, rinsed and drained

1 cup fresh or frozen corn, thawed

1 avocado, diced

½ cup diced sweet red pepper

½ cup coarsely chopped cilantro

¼ cup diced celery

2 green onions, trimmed and thinly sliced (about ¼ cup)

Procedure

Whisk together lemon juice, mustard, salt, pepper, and olive oil in large bowl.

Add all remaining ingredients, and gently toss to combine. Yield: 4 servings.

Nutrition Facts

Serving size: ¼ recipe (about 9 oz)

Amount Per Serving	
Calories	341.06
Calories From Fat (36%)	121.92
	% Daily Value
Total Fat 14.24g	22%
Saturated Fat 1.95g	10%
Cholesterol 0mg	0%
Sodium 247.51mg	10%
Potassium 696.28mg	20%
Total Carbohydrates 49.37g	16%
Fiber 8.86g	35%
Sugar 3.48g	
Protein 6.28g	13%

Cranberry Spinach Salad

1 tbsp olive oil

3/4 cup almonds, blanched and slivered

1/3 cup fructose

2 tsp minced onion

¼ tsp paprika

¼ cup white wine vinegar

¼ cup cider vinegar

1 Tbsp garlic clove, minced

½ cup olive oil

1 lb spinach, rinsed and torn into bite-size pieces

1 cup dried cranberries

2 tbsp toasted sesame seeds

1 tbsp poppy seeds

Procedure

Sauté almonds in butter for 2-3 minutes. In a large bowl, whisk agave, onion, paprika, vinegar, garlic and olive oil. Add remaining ingredients and toss to coat. Serve immediately. Yield: 8 servings

Nutrition Facts

Serving size: 1/8 recipe (about 7 oz)

Amount Per Serving	
Calories	533.94
Calories From Fat (40%)	215.93
	% Daily Value
Total Fat 24.91g	38%
Saturated Fat 2.69g	13%
Cholesterol 3.82mg	1%
Sodium 49.11mg	2%
Potassium 489.52mg	14%
Total Carbohydrates 75.7g	25%
Fiber 8.07g	32%
Sugar 9.51g	
Protein 5.21g	10%

Vegetarian Salads

Holiday Salad

4 ea hard boiled, cage free eggs, peeled and sliced
1 ea Romaine lettuce, torn into small chunks
1 ea red leaf lettuce, torn into small chunks
1 head Belgian endive, torn into small chunks
½ ea English cucumber, chopped
1 ea red bell pepper, chopped
1 ½ cup cherry tomatoes cut into quarters
1 ½ cup white mushrooms, sliced
1/8 cup balsamic vinegar
1/8 cup olive oil
¼ tsp ground black pepper
1 pinch salt

Procedure

Toss all ingredients together in a large bowl and serve immediately.

Yield: 12 servings

Nutrition Facts

Serving size: 1/12 recipe (about 7 oz)

Amount Per Serving	
Calories	78.59
Calories From Fat (49%)	38.54
	% Daily Value
Total Fat 4.35g	7%
Saturated Fat 0.88g	4%
Cholesterol 70.5mg	24%
Sodium 72.01mg	3%
Potassium 453.97mg	13%
Total Carbohydrates 6.58g	2%
Fiber 3.37g	13%
Sugar 1.96g	
Protein 4.27g	9%

Dandelion and Quorn Salad

4 tbsp chopped fresh tarragon
4 cloves garlic, minced (2 tsp.)
1 cup lemon juice
½ cup olive oil
4 Quorn patties, chopped into ¼" chunks
2 cups dandelion greens, thick stems trimmed
2 cups chicory leaves, outer ribs discarded, leaves torn into 2- inch pieces
2 cups baby arugula
1 medium Belgian endive, sliced into ½-inch-   thick rings (1 cup)
1 medium carrot, grated (½ cup)
1 small fennel bulb, thinly sliced (½ cup)
¼ cup thinly sliced celery
¼ cup chopped parsley
  Dash cayenne pepper

Procedure

Place tarragon, lemon juice, olive oil and garlic in a bowl. Whisk together.
Place ½ of the dressing in a Ziplock bag. Add the Quorn and shake well.
Cook the Quorn in a non-stick pan for 5-6 minutes until heated through.
Combine Quorn, dandelion greens, chicory, arugula, endive, carrot, fennel, celery, and parsley in large bowl.
Pour the remaining dressing on top and mix well.
Serve immediately.
Yield: 4 servings

Nutrition Facts

Serving size: ¼ recipe

Amount Per Serving	
Calories	435.21
Calories From Fat (63%)	272.57
	% Daily Value
Total Fat 30.84g	47%
Saturated Fat 4.28g	21%
Cholesterol 1.26mg	<1%
Sodium 538.22mg	22%
Potassium 1086mg	31%
Total Carbohydrates 29.22g	10%
Fiber 10.93g	44%
Sugar 4.83g	
Protein 16.21g	32%

Trinity Kale Salad

8 leaves each of curly kale, Russian kale and dino kale (shredded)

1 cup cherry tomatoes halved

4 ea hard boiled eggs, diced

1 tomato (diced)

1 avocado (diced)

3 tbsp onion (diced)

2-3 tbsp olive oil

2 tbsp agave nectar

4 tbsp lemon juice

sea salt to taste

Procedure

Combine olive oil, lemon juice, salt and agave in the bottom of a large bowl. Whisk well.

Combine all other ingredients in the bowl. Mix well.

Chill for 2 hours before serving.

Yield: 4 servings

Nutrition Facts

Serving size: ¼ recipe

Amount Per Serving	
Calories	380.03
Calories From Fat (58%)	219.41
	% Daily Value
Total Fat 24.86g	38%
Saturated Fat 5.87g	29%
Cholesterol 576.64mg	192%
Sodium 244.4mg	10%
Potassium 743.04mg	21%
Total Carbohydrates 21.84g	7%
Fiber 4.54g	18%
Sugar 11.85g	
Protein 19.69g	39%

Index

CPSIA information can be obtained
at www.ICGtesting.com
Printed in the USA
LVHW041521081020
668326LV00013B/1494